CHRISTS

CHRISTS

MEDITATIONS ON ARCHETYPAL IMAGES IN CHRISTIAN THEOLOGY

Volume I

David L. Miller

The Seabury Press-New York

1981
The Seabury Press
815 Second Avenue
New York, N.Y. 10017

Printed in the United States of America

Library of Congress Cataloging in Publication Data

Miller, David LeRoy.
    Christs: meditations on archetypal images in
Christian theology.

    Bibliography
    1. Jesus Christ—Person and offices—
Meditations. I. Title.
BT202.M525   232   80-25672
ISBN 0-8164-0492-5

ACKNOWLEDGMENTS

EARLIER versions of Parts I and III of this book, here in considerably amplified form, were given at the Eranos Conferences in Ascona, Switzerland, in 1977 and 1978. Those former versions are available in the Eranos Yearbooks, and are used by permission of the organizers of the Eranos meetings.

Part II was given in an earlier form at the Panarion Conference in Los Angeles in 1978. It has been completely recast for this volume and is used with the knowledge of the Panarion Foundation.

Grateful acknowledgment is made to the following publishers for permission to use the material listed:

Avon Books for excerpts from THE CLOWN by Heinrich Böll; copyright 1975 by Avon Books.

Doubleday & Company, Inc. for "The Song," copyright 1955 by Theodore Roethke from the book THE COLLECTED POEMS OF THEODORE ROETHKE; for excerpts from THE ODYSSEY by Homer, translated by Robert Fitzgerald, copyright 1961 by Robert Fitzgerald; for excerpt from "Summer Knowledge" by Delmore Schwartz, copyright 1959 by Modern Poetry Association; for excerpts from "The Kingdom of Poetry" by Delmore Schwartz, copyright 1958 by Delmore Schwartz, both from the book SUMMER KNOWLEDGE by Delmore Schwartz. Reprinted by permission of Doubleday & Company, Inc.

Drama Book Specialists for excerpts from THE FANTASTICKS/ CELEBRATION by Tom Jones and Harvey Schmidt, copyright 1973 by Drama Book Specialists (Publishers), (p. 42).

Harcourt Brace Jovanovich, Inc. for excerpts from THE COL- LECTED POEMS by T. S. Eliot; copyright 1963 by Harcourt Brace Jovanovich.

Alfred Knopf, Inc., Liveright Division, for excerpts from COL- LECTED POEMS by Wallace Stevens, copyright 1975 by Alfred Knopf, Inc; and for excerpts from OPUS POSTHUMOUS by Wallace Stevens, copyright 1977 by Alfred Knopf, Inc.

W. W. Norton & Company, Inc., Liveright Division, for excerpts from DEAR JUDAS AND OTHER POEMS by Robinson Jeffers; copyright 1977 by W. W. Norton & Company, Inc., Liveright Division.

Robert Payne for excerpt from THE WHITE PONY.

Random House, Inc, Modern Library Division for excerpt from SELECTED POETRY by William Blake; copyright 1953 by Random House, Inc.

New Directions Publishing Corp. for excerpt from SELECTED POEMS: SUMMER KNOWLEDGE by Delmore Schwartz; copyright 1967 by New Directions Publishing Corp.

Signet Books, The New American Library for excerpts from TRIS- TRAM SHANDY by Laurence Sterne, copyright 1962 by The New American Library.

Wesleyan University Press for excerpt from POEMS 1957–1967 by James Dickey; copyright 1967 by Wesleyan University Press.

The Viking Press for excerpts from FINNEGANS WAKE by James Joyce; copyright 1939 by James Joyce.

A WORD OF GRATITUDE

I SHOULD like to express my thanks to those persons who, often without knowing it, and sometimes very indirectly, have stimulated ideas in this book: Tori Potts Beattie, Ernst Benz, Henry Corbin, Patricia Cox, James Hillman, Stanley Romaine Hopper, Toshihiko Izutsu, James Karman, Magda Kcrényi, Ken Neuman, Richard Pilgrim, Steven Simmer, Huston Smith, Richard Underwood, and James Wiggins.

There are doubtless others who should be named, those whose subtle influences I have failed to notice. There come to mind all the students in graduate seminars at Syracuse University where, from 1976 to 1979, the ideas here recorded have been worked and reworked many times.

Most especially I am grateful to the hosts of the Eranos Conferences in Switzerland, particularly to Rudolf Ritsema, and to the entire Eranos Circle, who supported this work when its author had considerable doubt.

Finally, I am indebted in the extreme to Susan Schwartz, who labored diligently over the preparation of the manuscript.

The clowns in this book, the stories and images, the quiet and not-so-quiet tears and laughter, but especially all the love deeply felt and suffered here—
are dedicated to two most
amazing and wonderful persons:

Dianna & John

". . . of such is the Kingdom of God."

TABLE OF CONTENTS

Introduction: The Idea of a Polytheistic, Archetypal Theology
xv

PART ONE: CHRIST, THE GOOD SHEPHERD

PART TWO: CHRIST, THE CLOWN

INTRODUCTION   THE IDEA OF A POLYTHEISTIC, ARCHETYPAL THEOLOGY

IT BEGINS—as it will also end—with a poem. This is not only to indicate that things are better said poetically, though that of course is also true, but rather to express the view that some things can be said, if at all, only in image, metaphor, and likeness, as if

> We live in a constellation
> Of patches and of pitches,
> Not in a single world,
> In things said well in music,
> On the piano, and in speech,
> As in a page of poetry—
> Thinkers without final thoughts
> In an always incipient cosmos,
> The way, when we climb a mountain,
> Vermont throws itself together.[1]

That this first volume, first of several more to come, begins a project of "patches and pitches," yet a "constellation," not some "single world," lacking as it will always be in "final thoughts," will be perhaps all too obvious. But, like Everest, it must be climbed because it is there, and whether or not, like Vermont, it will throw *itself* together, remains to be seen . . .

Nonetheless it begins, as we were saying, with a poem. For what better introduction could there be to this work and to those to come than the second part of Wallace Stevens' poem, "The Owl and the Sarcophagus."

> There came a day, there was a day—one day
> A man walked living among the forms of thought
> To see their lustre truly as it is
>
> And in harmonius prodigy to be,
> A while, conceiving his passage as into a time
> That of itself stood still, perennial,
>
> Less time than place, less place than thought of place
> And, if of substance, a likeness of the earth,
> That by resemblance twanged him through and through,
>
> Releasing an abysmal melody,
> A meeting, an emerging in the light,
> A dazzle of remembrance and of sight.[2]

In the case of this work, the particular "forms of thought" are those of Christian theology. Whatever else may appear to be the case, this project intends to be *theology*, a *theologia* in the original sense of the stories and images of the gods. It means to be a re-visioning of Christianity's traditional "forms of thought." These "forms" consist, of course, in doctrines, teachings, and beliefs. Unfortunately, it is not every day that one walks "living" through these forms, as Stevens' poem says. They seem often to have lost their "lustre." But, perhaps, "there comes a day."

It is the faith of this project's experiment to suppose that the "lustre" is nonetheless still there, if one could only see it "as" it "is." The lively *images* (the as-forms) lying dormant and well-hidden in the doctrines, teachings, and beliefs have, perhaps, become unconscious or forgotten. Yet there is a "prodigy" in theology: prodigious, polytheistic myth-themes, archetypal motifs, lively images of a "perennial" sort in all the deepest religious ideas.

The "substance" of such forms are, as the poem says, "likenesses" of life. Their "resemblance" to our everyday reality "twangs" us "through and through." But the resonances may go unnoticed, may even be repressed, by tradition's ways of viewing. There is an "abysmal melody" waiting to be "released," which if it were made explicit might result in religion's "forms" seeming more realistic than we may have thought. As Stevens says in another peom, there is a "pale pole of resemblances / Experienced yet not well seen."[3]

It is the work of this work to attempt to "see" a bit better what we dimly "experience" as "resemblance" to life in the images of our faith. We live in a "constellation" of religious "patches and pitches," indeed. Theology in our time seeks the "Vermont" that, by some grace of valley if not mountain, "throws itself together" in everyday life-experience.

The *possibility* of reconstructing the relation between Christian theology's forms of thought and a person's life-experience was already argued in an earlier book, *The New Polytheism*.[4] That work was meant to be a sort of *prolegomenon* for the project of which this volume is the beginning.

The argument, put briefly, was as follows. Two commonplaces were observed. (1) From the second century to the twentieth, Christian theologians have thought it obvious that when the Church Fathers wanted to articulate the faith in reasonable ways they borrowed Greek philosophical thought-forms, which were the only ways of thinking available to them at that time. They put the content of the Gospel into that framework. (2) Scholars of Greek philosophy, meanwhile, have taken it to be just as obvious, as Aristotle had already confessed, that philosophy's ways of thinking were borrowed from the poets and myth-makers which served as the only context of expression for their time. Aristotle said that philosophical concepts and logics were just another vocabulary, now formal and logical, for the mythopoetic stories of the gods as told by Homer and Hesiod.[5]

These two commonplaces suggest a conclusion that, though seldom drawn, is both astonishing and promising. If behind the forms in which Christian doctrines have been thought, there are the concepts and categories, the ways of thinking and logics of Greek philosophy, *and* if behind the concepts and logics of that philosophy are the imaged stories and well-made plots of mythology, then hidden in the *forms* of Christian thinking, two times removed, are the gods and goddesses of ancient Greece! The implication is that the *monotheistic theology* of Christianity has many meanings living in it, a rich multifaceted constellation of possibilities whose articulation corresponds to the *polytheistic mythology* of classical Greece.

Not only is this surprising, but it is also promising. The images and rhythms of stories often seem to have a life-immediacy which intellectual concepts and rational logics do not. The tales are concrete, whereas the philosophy is abstract. A re-mythologizing of the doctrines, beliefs, and teachings of the Christian faith might bring to awareness the hidden possibilities of meaning, the concrete and plural sense of significance, the "pale pole of resemblances experienced yet not well seen." Such was the argument of the former book, and it is the hypothesis guiding this work and the ones to follow in this series.

Traditionally, as Anselm once said, theology is *fides quaerens intellectum,* "faith seeking understanding." The tradition of Western Christian theology has given us many "understandings" through the nearly two-thousand-year course of its history. The theology of this project has a different goal: not "faith seeking understanding," but theology's many understandings seeking life-sense. T. S. Eliot was perhaps pointing to this purpose in his poem, *Four Quartets,* when he wrote:

We had the experience but missed the meaning,
And approach to the meaning restores the experience
In a different form, beyond any meaning
We can assign to happiness.[6]

From the point of view of this work the poet might also have said: "We had the meanings but missed the experience."

C. G. Jung once noted that it is not an easy "undertaking to discover connecting links between dogma and immediate experience."[7] But that it may be important is indicated dramatically in a letter this psychologist wrote to Sigmund Freud in February, 1910. Jung hoped that there could be

> revivified among intellectuals a feeling for symbol and myth, ever so gently to transform Christ back into the soothsaying god of the vine which he was, and in this way absorb those ecstatic instinctual forces of Christianity for the one purpose of making the cult and the myth what they once were—a drunken feast of joy where man regained the ethos and holiness of an animal. That was the beauty and purpose of classical religion, which from God knows what temporary biological needs has turned into a Misery Institute. Yet what infinite rapture and wantonness lies dormant in our religion, waiting to be led back to their true destination! A genuine and proper ... development ... must bring to fruition ... the agony and ecstasy over the dying and resurgent god, the mythic power of the wine, the awesome anthropophagy of the Last Supper—only this ... development can serve the vital forces of religion.[8]

To "serve the vital forces of religion" by locating crucial images in theological ideas and "leading them back to their true destination": this is indeed the purpose of the work.[9] It has three dimensions.[10]

1. The first aspect of the work is to locate crucial ideas and to connect them with their fundamental images. This involves research in traditional Biblical and Historical Theology. Specifically, it is *Christology* which is the central notion of this volume. The images of the theology of Christ which are probed have to do with "Good Shepherd" (Part I), "Holy Fool" (Part II), and "Great Teacher" (Part III).

But the locating of the images in the theological ideas is not only a historical and Biblical task. The perspective here is rather to view such images as *archetypal*. By this is meant just what the word originally implied. *Typos* denoted the imprint made by a sculpted ring when it was pressed on warm wax. It has to do with the forms of pressure and suggests noting where a person is im-pressed or de-pressed. It has to do with what strikes one. To add the prefix, *archē*, deepens the idea. It is not just any striking or impression, but rather the most fundamental, archaic, deepest, most original one. Thus, viewed as *archetypal theology*, which is one way to think of this project, there is an attempt to deal with the images within theological ideas where they press on the life of the self or *psychē* ("soul") most profoundly. It means to be a soul-theology. Thus, in addition to being Historical and Biblical Theology, it is also a Psychology of Religion.

2. As one begins to probe the variety of images experienced in religious ideas there will emerge a likeness to ancient themes. It is then that re-mythologization occurs and then that the conclusion drawn from theological and philosophical assumptions will be, if at all, substantiated: behind the images of the doctrines, *all* the gods and goddesses!

For example, in this volume we will see that behind the doctrine of Christ who is thought of in the image of the Good Shepherd, there is not only Pan, the god of "pastoral" care, but also Polyphemos, the one-eyed monster. Behind Christ the Great Teacher is not only Socrates, but also Silenos lying drunk in a deep cave of myth. The instances will multiply as the work goes on. As they do it will be seen that this is not only an archetypal theology but, by virtue of its multiplicity, also *polytheistic*.

3. But the work is not yet complete when ideas are led back into fundamental imagery and when that imagery is deepened by reference to universal and transpersonal motifs of myth. There is still the matter of linking these collective, hidden

motifs to life-experience here and now. Wallace Stevens wrote not only of "remembrance" but also of "resemblance." There is therefore a third aspect to the work.

This third aspect was mentioned only obliquely in *The New Polytheism*, but it is crucial to the whole. The Church Fathers called it the task of turning image into likeness. The Book of Genesis, they pointed out, had said that God would create man "in our own image, after our likeness" (Genesis 1:26). But when it spoke of God actually doing the work of creation, only the former is mentioned. It says: "in his image." The Bible neglects to add the word "likeness" (Genesis 1:27). So the theologian, Origen, for example, writes: "Man received the honor of God's image in his first creation, whereas the completion of God's likeness was reserved . . . for his own earnest efforts." [11]

It is in this final "earnest effort" that the poet is an ally. It is in his craft that there is a "waking of a likeness within us." [12] The poet is at home in the work of discovering the metaphoric connections to life of fundamental images. Thus, this work conspires with those forms of thinking that cannot be accomplished without poetry, without image's metaphoric power. This means that the work is not only archetypal, involving Biblical and Historical matters psychologically; it is not only polytheistic, involving researches and methods in History of Religions and Comparative Mythology, but it is finally *theopoetic*,[13] with a gratitude to so many modern studies in Religion and Literature.

Thus, in this volume it will not be enough to see in ideas about Christ the gods of Greece—Silenos, Polyphemos, and all the rest.[14] It is also crucial to see what these gods want with us today, what they are doing in our lives. So the images, the shades of the gods, will be explored in their contemporary imaginal versions: the "shepherd" in Shakespeare and Eliot, in Robinson Jeffers, James Dickey, and Theodore Roethke; the "fool" in Heinrich Böll and James Joyce, in Lawrence Sterne and Nikolai Gogol; the "teacher" in Hopkins and Hoffmann, in

Baudelaire, Rimbaud, and Verlaine. In the powerful poetry of these writers, as well as in many others, we may get an intimate sense of how fundamental christological images are impinging on human experience today. In this way we shall have attempted to sense the "likeness" in life of theological ideas.

Nor is the work complete in Christian forms of thought with the exploration only of the various images of Christ, the variety of "christs" which, as the poet Hopkins said, "christ in us." Future volumes in this series of archetypal meditations will deal with "Trinities" (Volume II), "Holy Ghosts" (Volume III), "Kingdoms of God" (Volume IV), "Life after Deaths" (Volume V), and "Resurrections of the Soul of Body" (Volume VI). Each of these books in the total project is meant to be yet another moment in a *theologia imaginalis* ("an imaginal theology") . . . which calls to mind one final matter by way of introduction.

Already in *The New Polytheism* there was a warning against two possible misunderstandings of the task. "The work," it was there written, "is not to find allegorical typologies: it is not to make clever associations between far-fetched correspondences. Nor is the work historical: a genetic tracing of the connections which exist in the conscious evolution of thinking, from mythology to philosophy to theology. The first task would be trivial; and the second, even were it possible, would be irrelevant to our purpose. The real task is something other, and it cannot be satisfied by some academic chore, however well performed, even were the effort worth it. The task rather is . . . to recover the varieties of religious experience lurking in the varieties of theological ideas. The task begins in feeling and intuition, rather than in thinking." [15]

The point of this was meant to be the same as that of Henry Corbin. He speaks of *mundus imaginalis* (an "imaginal world"), translating the Sufi notion of *'ālam al-mithāl*. This is a realm *between* that of the mind and that of experience, between idea and reality, between ideal and real, between infinite and finite, between God and man. It is a "middle realm," a *metaxy*, as

Plato put it. In the world of *images* (*phantasiai*, said the Greeks),[16] things are both mindful and passionate, both ideal and real, infinite but very present, divine and human at once. To move in that realm is intellectual, in the way that we are all thinkers, but it is also and at the same time a matter of heart-felt reality.

This work, in so far as it manages to be *theologia imaginalis*, is not merely intellectual ("clever associations") nor is it merely historical ("tracings in the evolution of consciousness"). It speaks, if at all, out of an "other" place which is nonetheless a "place" we all know all too well, even if dimly. It is, as Stevens said, a "likeness of the earth," a "resemblance" that "twangs us through and through." If seeing the "likenesses" of a *theologia imaginalis* involves a "release of an abysmal melody," or a "sombre figuration," it may nonetheless occasion a rebirth of religious meaning.[17]

"Sombre figuration" is a phrase from another of Stevens' poems. These lines from that poem sum up the ideas of this Introduction:

> *There is a man whom rhapsodies of change,*
> *Of which he is the cause, have never changed*
> *And never will, a subman under all*
> *The rest, to whom in the end the rest return,*
> *The man below the man below the man,*
> *Steeped in night's opium, evading day.*

This is to say that the work of a *theologia imaginalis* is, in fact, in the deep self ("subman"). It is a work which touches that which is perennial in our thinking, images to which we, willy nilly, "return" in the end.

> *We have grown weary of the man that thinks.*
> *He thinks and it is not true . . .*

This is the merely rationalistic theologian who even when orthodox and correct somehow does not manage to be "true" to our sense of everyday life. But . . .

> *. . . the man below*
> *Imagines and it is true, as if he thought*
> *By imagining, anti-logician, quick*
> *With a logic of transforming certitudes.*
> *It is not that he was born in another land,*
> *Powdered with primitive lights and lives with us*
> *In glimpses, on the edge or at the tip,*
> *Playing a crackled reed, wind-stopped, in bleats.*

That is, it is not that mythology's depth to theology's ideas lives only archaically in some ancient historic time long gone. Rather . . .

> *He was born within us as a second self,*
> *A self of parents who have never died.*
> *Whose lives return, simply upon our lips.*
> . . . .
> *He dwells below, the man below, in less*
> *Than body and in less than mind, ogre.*
> *Inhabitant, in less than shape, of shapes*
> *That are dissembled in vague memory*
> *Yet still retain resemblances, remain*
> *Remembrances . . .*

And then Stevens' lines tell us that such depths of self "turn us into scholars, studying / The masks of music" which "glisten / With meanings" that are "discerned / In the beat of the blood." [18]

Here then is the "place" of a *theologia imaginalis:* neither in the rational mind alone, nor merely in historical and personal experiences. Rather, it is "in the beat of blood." It is indeed to the end of such vital rhythms, those as near to us as our very life-blood, that this present work follows Stevens, as well as so many before him, in the clue: "The man below beholds . . . an image." [19] In this book it is the images of Christ: the "christs" sensed in the ideas and in the life of "the man below."

PART ONE | CHRIST, THE GOOD SHEPHERD

1 PERFECTIONISM AND THE IMITATIO CHRISTI

> *"You, therefore, must be perfect, as
> your heavenly Father is perfect."*
> —MATTHEW 5:48 (RSV)

HOW is this possible? *Imitatio dei!* Who could be like God?
The very Gospel which attributes the perfectionist commandment to Jesus also informs us that "no one is good but God." [1]
And the religious tradition in which these sayings are found
asserts that there is an "infinite qualitative distinction" between
man and God. To ask of man that he be perfect like a God who
is ultimately different from him is, on the face of it, an impossible obligation. We are double-bound from the beginning.

Alan Watts has suggested that the impossible commandment
to perfection was what in the Orient is called spiritual *upaya,* a
bit of teaching trickery, an intentional pedagogical technique
designed to help us let go of heroic pretensions to grace. In
unending vain attempts to achieve ultimate meaning for our
lives we would at last realize the impossibility of the bind, give
up in our ego-efforts, and thereby allow that-which-is to come
on its own. [2]

Watts may be "right," but his way of explaining things sounds somehow more like Hindu Vedanta or Zen Buddhist than it does Western Christian. The Johannine literature, for example, confirms the enigma of Matthew. In the Fourth Gospel we read: "Your joy may be perfected" (John 16:24), and in the Epistle: "Everyone who abideth in Him does not sin" (I John 3:6). Paul, too, affirms that "when the perfect comes, the imperfect will pass away" (I Corinthians 13:10). And the writer of the Book of Hebrews gives Moses, Abraham, Isaac, Jacob, and Christ, whom he calls the High Priest, as examples of a perfection after which Christians should strive.[3]

Theological interpretations of the New Testament have a tone different from that of Oriental religions which indeed support Watts' view and that of Yoshida Kenkō who, in the thirteenth-century *Essays in Idleness*, could write: "Leaving something incomplete makes it interesting," as for example the crucial imperfections worked into vases from the Ming Dynasty.[4] Clement of Alexandria seems more to the point of Western theology when he mused: "It is a thing impossible that man should be perfect as God is perfect; but it is the Father's will that we, living according to the Gospel in blameless or unfailing obedience, should become perfect."[5] On this Passmore writes: "Jesus . . . lays it down that men are to perfect themselves. Since he would not behave so absurdly as to command men to become what they are in fact incapable of becoming, it follows, on the face of it, that men must be able to perfect themselves."[6] Though Passmore attributes this view to Pelagius, a Christian heretic, the view is nonetheless typical of much Church theology in the West, not to mention popular piety.

This is no small matter. Varieties of religious perfectionism, however suspect of heresy, have been insisted upon by Clement of Rome and Clement of Alexandria, by Polycarp, Ignatius, and Irenaeus, by Catholic and Protestant pietistic and mystical movements, by Quakerism and Methodism, by British Ranters and by the American Oneida Community—to name only a few!

Furthermore, the worrying of the perfectionist double-bind by the theological tradition has been a source of some of the most central and difficult debates in religious history. For example, there were Augustine against the Pelagians; the controversy of faith and works, especially in the case of Luther against the Roman Church; justification differentiated from sanctification; the relation of the "persons" of the Trinity; sacramental orthodoxism struggling against communitarianism; warring at the Council of Trent; Arminian and liberal theologians fighting neo-orthodoxy and existentialism; and so on.[7]

In the subtleties of these schisms are reflected the duplicity of the perfectionist commandment, the experience of the schizophrenic quality of the Gospel. On the one hand, the ever-so-popular Methodists, Wesley and Fletcher, imply that the religious man can and ought to achieve perfection consciously in life. Wesley says: "By perfection I mean the humble, gentle, patient love of God and our neighbor, ruling our tempers, words, and actions."[8] But in so saying, he and others like him come close to the Pelagian heresy condemned at the Council of Carthage. Thus, such as Augustine, Luther, Calvin, and Barth vigorously deny the possibility of perfection as a result of human effort. These men affirm what Paul Tillich called the "divine-demonic ambiguity" as being an integral part of, rather than being transcended by, the religious life.[9]

Nonetheless, the Wesleyans and their ilk, rather than the more main-line theologians, won the popular religious imagination of the West. The people persist in supposing that being Christian has something to do with perfecting life, interpreting this morally in relation to behavior with others and in relation to feelings about one's self. A literal understanding of the text from Matthew is at the center of an Occidental way of seeing life. Augustine may have had the "right opinion" of ortho-doxy on his side, but Pelagius' spirit has reigned supreme in the soul of a double-bound populace. Esoteric doctrinal controversies of theologians—faith versus works, and the like—are not only theological debates. They are psychic wars lived in the soul of everyman.

This matter does not end with those who are self-consciously devout. Secular life, too, has been firmly under the domination of a perfectionist obligation which, whether orthodox or heretic, is consistently religious in content and tone. It is the perfectionist predicament about which Sigmund Freud wrote when, in his work on culture, he notes that an obsession to perfect civilization brings with it a deep discontent. In a historical work on the history of Western perfectionism, Passmore lists other cultural symptoms of the compulsion, such as Utopian fantasies and hopes, from Plato to B. F. Skinner; Nazi ideas and Marxism; American varieties of technological mastery; the spirituality of Teilhard de Chardin and Maharishi Mahesh Yogi; Erich Fromm's humanism and Timothy Leary's drug culture.[10]

We feel everywhere and always the obligation to be perfect, if not now, at least in some indeterminate or metaphysical future. Even our imperfections are ruled by a perfectionist sense. We imagine the war that will "make the world safe for democracy"; the "great train robbery," perfect in every minute detail; or the perfect love affair, an illicit liaison whose excitement and sex will be at last ultimately satisfying. The American vernacular puts the perfectionist theme succinctly: "You're going to do it, and do it, 'till you do it right!"

Reformations and theological councils will come and go, but our religiosity is perfectionist, if heretically so, and our secular life is unwittingly religious, fanatic in its various compulsions. However much theological sleight-of-tongue the doctors of the Church may provide—such as saying that the commandment in Matthew is eschatological rather than moral in its intention, or that perfection comes as a divine gift rather than as a human accomplishment, or that all men are already perfected in the work of Christ—the fact remains that we feel what we feel.

We sense life as an unending series of "shoulds" and

"oughts" and "musts." We not only *dream the impossible dream*," but we attempt vainly and with futility to act it out, employing rational consciousness, technological muscle, and a Protestant style that is typical of the American frontier.[11]

There may yet be a final irony to the discontent that Western civilization senses in its perfectionist soul. One little word— *teleios* ("perfect")—seems to have controlled man's sense. But this word in Matthew's saying is not used in Luke's version of Jesus' utterance. In the Third Gospel we read: "Be merciful as your Father is merciful" (Luke 6:36). There is nothing about perfection here at all. Scholars such as Wellhausen, Marriott, and Creed have, through intricate literary and textual studies, judged the Lucan form to be more original. The Judaizing writer of the First Gospel may have been trying to show how Jesus' saying matches Jewish scripture in Deuteronomy 18.13 ("Be blameless before the Lord your God"), where the word "blameless" is rendered by *teleios* in the Septuagint's Greek version of the Hebrew Bible. In fact, the Greek word *teleios* was customarily reserved for references to the gods. Men were hardly thought to be *teleios*, "perfect." So the obligation for man to be perfect, as implied by the Gospel of Matthew, may well be a bit of editorial enthusiasm. The irony of our pervasive perfectionism is that it may all be a mistake![12]

2 THE GOOD SHEPHERD AND HIS SHEEP

A POWERFUL archetypal image reinforces the double-binding discontent of perfection's sense. The Book of Hebrews uses the figure of Christ as High Priest for the paradigm of perfection in life, and, in the benediction to this Book, the High Priest (Christ) is identified as "the shepherd of the sheep" (Hebrews 13:20). Similarly, in the early Christian work, *The Shepherd of Hermas,* it is a shepherd who tells the author in a vision to "perfect his ministry" (*telein diakonian*). As in Hebrews, the term for perfection (*teleios*) is connected to the work of a shepherd.[1] The implication is that the shepherd is a fundamental image of the sense of perfection. The classical location of this notion is eighteen verses in the tenth chapter of the Gospel of John.

In the pericope of the Good Shepherd, a shepherd is contrasted with a thief who does not enter the fold by the door (verses 1–2). The shepherd is himself referred to as being a door by which one may enter the fold (verse 7). He calls the sheep by their right names and they know who he is (verse 3). He leads them (verse 4). He gives the sheep life and saves them from death (verses 9–10). He even dies for the sheep (verses 9, 17–18). And the shepherd refers to himself as being "good," using a word in Greek, *kalos,* which ordinarily means "beautiful" (verse 14). Such are the traits of the Good Shepherd.

The implications are clear. To be a shepherd is to be good. To be good one ought to be a shepherd. Following in such a path would make one a sheep and to follow perfectly, one must presume, would mean being a Paschal Lamb, pure and innocent, under the constant protective care of the shepherd, even though the lamb, so perfected, will be slaughtered precisely for being perfectly innocent.[2]

The Biblical image of the perfect Lamb who, in *imitatio dei,* is at the same time a Good Shepherd of the One Flock, struck strongly in the historical iconographic imagination. The Praetextat Catacomb, for example, pictures a Good Shepherd protecting the flock from monstrous beasts. Other instances may be found in the Catacombs of Callixtus, Commodilla, Diomittilla, and Jordani. There seems to be a special fondness in this art for picturing the shepherd as carrying a lost sheep on his shoulders. Notable instances of this may be seen in the tomb of Aurelius, in the mausoleum of Galla Placidia in Ravenna, and in the tomb of Beratius Nicatoras in Asia Minor.[3]

In addition to the iconographic imagination of the Church, the liturgical tradition has carried the image of the shepherd in prominent ways. In the Prayer of General Confession, human imperfection is likened to "straying from Thy ways like lost sheep." The Preface to the Consecration (*hanc igitur*) in the Canon of the Mass reads: "We beseech Thee Lord . . . to deliver us from eternal damnation and to cause us to be numbered among the flock of the elect." The *Dies Irae* intones, on behalf of the one who has died, to "keep me with sheep and away from the goats." Surely Handel's oratorio has done not a little for popularizing this image: "He will feed his flock like a shepherd / He will gather the young lambs in his arms / He will carry them in his bosom." This brings to mind, not only the prophecy that it quotes, but also the twenty-third Psalm, about which Father Gerald Vann has written: "For three thousand years men have found comfort in this poetry and have steadied their souls in the praying of it in times of tribulation. Christianity," Father Vann concludes, "is a religion of joy because it teaches that sorrow can be turned to joy." [4] The point of being a sheep under the care of a shepherd seems to carry the implication of turning negative experience into some perfect end, some happy ending. The fantasy is pervasive.

Nor is it only Christian. Behind the Church's use of the image of the shepherd and his sheep is an association in the ancient world between shepherd and king. For example, in Sumeria, Babylonia, and Assyria, the king was thought of as a shepherd who was appointed by a god. In the languages of these peoples, the verb, "to pasture," meant "to rule (like a king)." In Egypt, also, pharoahs were called "shepherds," and they were linked to the god Osiris, who was shepherd of the underworld. A Pyramid Text reads: "Thou has taken them up in thine arms as a shepherd his flock." [5] The Greek poet Homer likewise makes the connection between shepherd and king when he speaks of Agamemnon as *poimēn laōn*, "shepherd of the people." [6] According to Plato's account in *The Republic*, Socrates and Thrasymachus converse about the ruler of the people, referring to this office in the state as that of a shepherd. [7] So it is that the image of the shepherd carries connotations of ruling and controlling.

The Bible picks up the motif of "ruling" from the ancient world, but moves the symbol of the shepherd in the direction of the idea of "protection," as if protecting is a way of controlling and ruling. To be sure, Jeremiah denotes political and military leads by the term "shepherd," [8] but more than this is attributed to the figure. The shepherd guides (Psalm 12:3). He leads to pasture and nourishes (Jeremiah 50:19). He gives rest beside still waters (Isaiah 40:11); protects with his staff (Psalm 23:4); and whistles to the dispersed gathering them into one flock, herding them together (Zechariah 10:8; Isaiah 56:8). In short, protection is the shepherd's work. So in John 21:15–19, we are told that the shepherd is obliged to "feed my lambs, tend my sheep."

The image has power and, like the sense of perfection which it supports, its domination has controlled secular as well as religious life in the West. The tenacity of the shepherd-ideal is witnessed, for example, in its hold on the imagination of the poetic tradition of the pastoral, from Hellenistic idylls of Theocritus and Bion, through Sidney, Spenser, Marlowe, and Raleigh in the sixteenth century, Shakespeare, Jonson, Marvel, and Fletcher in the seventeenth, Pope, Gay, and Swift in the eighteenth, to Shelley, Keats, Tennyson, and Yeats in nineteenth-century British verse.[9]

Yet the image of the shepherd in the interpretation and felt-judgments of everyday life is not always experienced in the way indicated by the poet's lines about the "passionate shepherd":

> Who can live in heart so glad
> As the merry country lad?[10]

"Merry" and "glad" are hardly words which describe the way in which the split archetype of Good Shepherd/Innocent Lamb actually functions when its full impact is felt in, say, marriage, parenting, teaching, the vocations of medicine and law, the ruling of governments, and therapy.

Under the domination of this fantasy one imagines that the good and perfect husband is one who shepherds his wife. She in turn is given sheep status. Her innocent lamb-ness, in its turn, is viewed as perfect when she shepherds home and children. And so it goes.

Meanwhile, business executive, priest, teacher, prime minister or president, doctor, lawyer, and analyst shepherd their various flocks. The flock imagines itself to be sheep in order to purchase the protection of some shepherd, and the shepherd achieves his self-understanding by relating to those who think of themselves as his sheep. But the protection is attained at a cost. The price is that the sheep—if we follow the fantasy—have only two alternatives: on the one hand, to be innocent lambs, slaughtered by an eternally inferior role; or, on the other hand, to be lost or black sheep.

Religion has given us a strange image by which we oblige ourselves to a sense of impossible perfection. Perhaps it is not without some reason that we should "beware of one who comes in sheep's clothing" (Matthew 7:15)—including those images which so come. C. G. Jung used the phrase "grotesque paradox" when speaking of the Johannine image of the lamb.[11] However socially useful the image may be to civilization, the Good Shepherd's goodness can be devastating to the psyche, stealing liberty like a thief, killing to the soul, like some monster slaughtering the sheep who thought they wanted care.

Jewish tradition seems already to have sensed the negative psychological function of the theological imagery, being, as it was, somewhat reticent concerning the shepherd. Rabbi Jose ben Chanina in the third century asked how God could be called a shepherd in the Psalms. Such persons, he said, are despicable.[12] A midrash on Psalm 23 says: "No position in the world is so despised as that of the shepherd."[13] A rabbinic list of thieving and cheating occupations included the shepherd! In fact, shepherds were denied civil rights in ancient times. To buy wool, milk, or a kid from a shepherd was forbidden on the assumption that it was stolen property.[14] God tells Zechariah, according to Scripture, that His anger is "hot against the shepherd." The prophet in turn tells the people that God will "strike the shepherd" and "scatter the sheep."[15] One Christian interpreter exclaims in desperation concerning this negative passage concerning the shepherd, "There is no more enigmatic section in the Bible."[16] Indeed, one may wonder, given the

Jewish background of the image, why the shepherd attains the powerful status that it does in Christian tradition. The answer, perhaps, is the fact of the Good Shepherd pericope in John's Gospel.

But this answer helps little, concealing, as it does, an irony which is not unlike that observed concerning perfection (page 7, above). Not only does the narrative of the Good Shepherd not find overwhelming prefiguration in Hebrew scripture, but it intrudes into the Johannine text itself. It interrupts a discourse about physical and spiritual blindness, not seeming to fit into the Gospel context. Especially troublesome about this intrusion are the following items: the shepherd here is a messiah, whereas in ancient literature he has been pictured as a king or military leader; motifs of the fold, the door, and the contrast with the thief have little or no Jewish precedent; and, most crucial of all, the reciprocal relationship between shepherd and sheep—he calling them by name and they knowing who he is—is alien to a religious tradition where God and man are "infinitely qualitatively distinct." For the shepherd to say, "I know (ginōskein) my own and they know me," suggests more gnosis ("knowledge") than pistis ("faith"). This leads Rudolf Bultmann, for one, to conclude that the Good Shepherd section must either be original with the particular author of this Gospel or it must have a source different from the Judaeo-Christian heritage.[17]

Such a source in fact exists! In Mandean Gnostic literature we read: "Have confidence in Mandā d'Haijē. Like a good shepherd who watches (his sheep), he will keep far from you all spirit of apostasy. Like a good shepherd who leads his sheep to their fold, he will set you down and plant you down before him." "I am a shepherd who loves his sheep." "My little sheep, my little sheep, come! Follow my call!" These texts go on to contrast shepherd and thief, picturing the former as a redeemer rather than king or military leader, and they even depict the shepherd as carrying the sheep on his shoulders![18]

The irony hidden in the fact that the Good Shepherd of the Fourth Gospel has been so theologically tenacious, even when psychologically double-binding, is that the whole supporting passage may be taken from a heretical source. It may be a case of a pervasive christology, impacting even on secular life, giving religious sanction to our sense of perfection and its obliging duties, yet being as alien to the religious tradition to which it is attributed as it is intimately stuck in popular imagination.

Yet even if it were all a mistake, it is a potent fantasy nonetheless. So much is this the case that the music master of Molière's Monsieur Jourdain can be made to exclaim: "Why always shepherds? One sees nothing but that everywhere." [19] And when Rosalind, in *As You Like It*, says: "This shepherd's passion / Is much upon my fashion," we can sympathize with the response of Touchstone, the clown: "And mine, but it grows somewhat stale with me." [20]

3 THE SHEPHERD'S SINGLE EYE AND IMITATIONS

THE image grows stale from time to time, or "sad," as Ben Jonson said of the shepherd.[1] Perhaps the reason for this waning has to do with implications in four different areas of life: namely, social behavior, a sense of self, religious understanding, and philosophical point of view.

1. The first implication has to do with the *imitatio dei* of Matthew's saying, "be perfect like God," and with the *imitatio christi* of the Johannine Good Shepherd. Whether it be a case of some "shepherd" trying to imitate God, or of a "sheep" following after its "shepherd," what is implied for a person's relationship to others is an ethics or sociology of imitation (*mimēsis*). In commenting on the theme of perfection in the writings of Philo, Walther Völker has said: "Perfection . . . means nothing other than the peak-experience of life (*Lebensgipfel*), where everything is in a form (*gestaltet wird*) of imitation of God (*mimēsis theou*)."[2]

Taking account of the mimēsis or *imitatio* in a shepherd-like sense of perfection may help to explain the feeling of double-bind, the discontent. Viewing life as an imitation leads me to feel that I am something that I am not, whether it be God or Christ, parent, teacher, friend, mate, therapist, or some other heroic ideal. Curiously, this imitation of an externalized "other" produces an inflation of one's own ego. For example, *imitatio christi,* taken literally or moralistically, can make for a spiritual pride, a sort of divinizing of ego which is now sensed as Christ-like. Another instance is Aristotle's version of what happens in the theatre. As an imitation of life's action, the drama seduces the audience into feeling a superiority to the pity and terror of the action on stage, even though that pity and terror may be fundamental to all lives. A third case is Plato's idealistic view of knowledge where, in the act of knowing, there is a *mimēsis* that identifies the knower with Being itself. When such mimetic obligation pervades my sociology or ethics, a great weight is felt on the shoulders, as if one were shouldering the whole flock.

2. The psychological implication of this is that the weight is none other than my own ego! Imitation is never as good as the "real" thing. The copy is never able to match the original. So, in *imitatio,* we perpetrate a self-deception upon ourselves. After inflating the ego with important personal identifications and transferences, using the standard tricks of moralism and idolatry, the perspective of *imitatio,* with its obligation to be perfect, leaves the self with an unending sense of inferiority. This is curious, is it not? The ego-perspective of a mimetic psychology is infected, precisely in trying to make itself superior (like Christ or Daddy), with an ineluctable inferiority. The best sheep of the Good Shepherd is, like the Suffering Servant himself, a lamb led to slaughter.

3. There is a theological side to this, too. John Passmore touches upon it when he notes how the *imitatio* that is implied in Matthew and John would have presented a problem to the polytheistic perspective of the ancient Greek. Socrates re-

minded Euthyphro that what was welcome to Zeus was not favored by Kronos; what was pleasing to Hephaistos was hateful to Hera; and so on. If *mimēsis* is the touchstone of our sociology and our psychology, then which god should one imitate?[3] Which Christ is our personal Lord and Savior?—the teacher or the preacher, the healer or the one who violates the Law, the Roman Catholic "Christ" or the Baptist "Christ," the Shepherd or the Lamb? In order to make workable the perspective of *imitatio* or *mimēsis*—whether we be mimes of God or Christ, of mortal hero or ideological ideal—there must be an implicit single-mindedness, an ego-moral-literalism, a theological monotheism.

This may be why Philo, writing on the perfectionist perspective of the Book of Hebrews, contrasts it with the imperfectionism of older revelations in which the central characteristics are multiplicity (*polytropos*) and manifoldness (*polymeros*). Polytropic man, Philo asserts, is imperfect because he "has many ends, is drawn in different directions, shaken, driven to confusion and unable to find fixity."[4] In the work, *De migratione Abrahami*, Philo writes: "The soul of the wicked man is multiple (*polytropos*)."[5] Similarly, *The Shepherd of Hermas* tells us: "They who are perfect in faith . . . are double-minded in nothing."[6]

4. In John Fletcher's eighteenth-century book, *Essay on Christian Perfection,* religious single-mindedness is connected to a fourth symptom of the shepherd's sense of perfection. "In order to be Christian," Fletcher writes, "perfection must also be the perfection of the pure intent, the single eye."[7] The visual metaphor here is crucial. By associating singleness of mind to the visual imagination, there is implied a way of knowing which is dependent upon a human faculty. But if understanding is dependent upon some faculty of the knowing-self, then meaning would have as its source some subject or some object (that is, the seer or the seen). In this perspective the meaning of meaning is either subjectivist and relativistic or objectivist and

thereby relying totally on images from outside. In this manner, a philosophy of the imagination whose controlling metaphor is the seeing eye implies that images are separate from the eye which sees them. Such a philosophy focuses on seeing images rather than on seeing imaginally.

It is certainly not accidental that the Gospel, which commands a perfection, *imitatio dei,* also tells us that "if your eye is sound, your whole body is full of light." [8] Nor is it surprising that the Ranters, a perfectionist movement in England, produced an important tract with the title, "A Single Eye, All Light." A mock-advertisement for the American perfectionist community in Oneida, New York, reads: "It is known that many persons with two eyes habitually 'see double.' To prevent stumbling and worse liabilities in such circumstances, an ingenious contrivance has been invented by which the *whole body* is filled with light. It is called the *'single eye,'* and may be obtained by applying to Jesus Christ." [9]

The perfection advertised by such daylight-solar-visual consciousness not only traps our sense of meaning in a hopeless Cartesian separation of subject and object,[10] but it also limits an imaginal approach to life, as is indicated in these sentences from the nineteenth-century work, *Dictionnaire des sciences philosophiques*: "Do you want to discover absolute perfection? Leave to one side the imagination with its laborious combinations." [11]

These four, then, are characteristics of the perfectionist obligation of the shepherd-image: (1) *mimēsis* or *imitatio* in morality; (2) an ego-perspective in the psyche; (3) monotheistic literalism and fundamentalism in religious understanding; and (4) rationalistic intellectualism in our single-minded ways of knowing. Each of these carries a shadow-side: inferiority, the weight of an inflated sense of ego, limitations on individualism and in imagination. Is it any wonder that the shepherd-ideal grows stale and, in fact, is a monstrous killer of soul and of social relationships?

Perhaps this is why the language of the street, the people's metaphors, are somewhat less than idealistic about the shepherd and his sheep. The tone of slang makes the point.

In Great Britain, a "sheep shearer" is a cheat or swindler, and a "sheep walk" is a prison. The colloquial speech of Australia says that land is "sheep sick" if it has been grazed too long. "Sheep wash" is inferior liquor in New Zealand. A retort to "Two heads are better than one," is, "Yes, even if one is a sheep's head." [12] In sixteenth-century England, it was common to say about wives, "One shrew is worth two sheep." Lyly, in 1580, wrote: "Although the virgin were somewhat shrewishe at first, yet in tyme she might become a Sheepe." And there is the phrase from Farrar's book, *Darkness and Dawn*: "The youth refused to kill himself with the sheeplike docility of so many of his contemporaries." Chapman's *All Fools* exclaims: "Kisse her you sheepshead." And we all know about "sheepishness," "wooly-mindedness," "being fleeced," "by hook or crook," "belonging to the herd," and having it "rammed down our throats." In 1900, R. H. Savage wrote about a couple of "California manipulators going over to London to shear those fatwitted sheep, the English investors." [13]

Language gives us the sense of it, the body and soul of perfectionism, the feeling when sheep and shepherd become bound to one another. The Good Shepherd, it would seem, casts a considerable shadow. The people do not take kindly to the double-bind, the discontent of his grotesque sense of perfection. Some betrayal is felt in the notion and its powerful image, some delusion and deception, some Judas. This is given expression by Charles Dickens' pickwickean sentence about a pastor of a Church: " 'The kiss of peace,' says the Shepherd, and then *he* kissed the *women* all round!" [14]

4 THE END OF PERFECTION

THE ideas of theology, with their lurking archetypal images, are as dangerous as drugs. They infect our social relationships and our psychology. They give form to our perspectives. The danger is all the greater because the function of theology in everyday life is often unconscious.

It is indeed the case that the christological imagination has been by its shepherd-imagery a sort of Judas-kiss, loading on man's shoulders a sense of impossible perfection. But in this imaginal work the Bible has had a co-conspirator aiding and abetting the sheepish sense.

When the Church Fathers needed to interpret the sayings about perfection in the New Testament, they typically borrowed a standard tradition from Greek philosophy. This commonplace explains the Greek word for perfection (*teleios*) by linking it to its cognate, *telos,* a term which means "end." Aeschylus and Herodotus, Plato and Aristotle, indeed, the classical tradition generally, reasoned that to be perfect is to be at the end, to end, happy ending. And to be at some end would be to be perfected.[1]

Language itself, on the other hand, may well know better than the Greek philosophers and the Christian theologians. The word, *telos,* did not always mean "end," though indeed it came to be used consistently in that way by a tradition which simultaneously elevated the notion of solar consciousness, the human ego, single-mindedness, and clear thinking. Onians has showed, for example, that it is impossible to translate *telos* by the word "end" in the following passage from *The Theogony* by Hesiod: "There was no loosing of the dire strife (*eris*), nor was there an end (*oude teleute*) for either side in the war; rather, the *telos* of the war was extended evenly."[2] If the war was *oude teleute* ("without end"), then the "*telos* of war" cannot mean the "end of the war."

In fact the notion of some "end" veils deeper and richer meanings of *telos* in the Greek language. In various early texts the term suggests: a "wrapping," like the cloud of death, the veil of dream, the covering on Hades' head, the bands of fate, the cloths which shroud a corpse; or "city walls," like those built by the Cyclopes at Tiryns; or a "hat" which one wears, especially those hats giving the person a vocational identification or destiny; or a "wheel of fortune"; a "wedding band," bonding two persons into one marriage; and even, a "crown" which circles the head of a boxing champion.[3]

These uses of the word imply a binding, tying it up or tying it down, like the *telos* of dying. The *telos* of *teleios,* the "end of perfection," may be viewed by the philosopher and the theologian to give man a *telos,* an "end," but the language tells a different story, a tale of binding and bondage. Like the wedding band, the hero's crown, the wheel of fortune, and the city walls, *teleios* is circular, without end, *ateleia,* the Greeks would say, "no end." The end (*telos*) of perfection (*teleios*) is endless (*ateleia*)!

This endlessness is likely to be sensed in life's vicious circles and double-binds, not as perfection at all, but as imperfection. This would indicate that Greek philosophical and Christian theological explanations which attempt to link perfection to *telos* are simply not in harmony with our actual experience. We fail always to be perfect—or so we imagine in the manner of some shepherd's sheep. The explanations that attempt to connect perfection and ends fail us by not providing a way of imagining our failure, a way of sensing *im*perfection.

Nor would it help much to use the idea of "original sin," or that of "evil as *privatio boni* ('privation of good')," or those of "Christ the Judge" and the "slaughtering of the innocent Lamb who died for our imperfection." All of these images of negative experience and feeling still depend upon some implicit notion of perfection, these ideas each being taken as opposite, thereby remaining in a perfectionist complex of meaning, for which, while feeling imperfect, being without end, we can get no sense.

Nor will it help in the matter of soul's depths to substitute the notion of completion for that of perfection, as Jung suggested, *if* in the process the new idea is not released from the fantasy of shepherd/sheep. It is this powerful fantasy that binds soul's life to a perfectionist complex by implying a preconceived idea of "end" (*telos*) or termination or health. This implication guarantees a sense of self which can never achieve what is expected. It is never-ending.[4] Integrating deep aspects of self or accepting shadow or getting in touch with one's feelings or making the unconscious conscious, all in some set program of therapy, would be, however secular, yet another performance of religiously shepherding sheep, or of being sheep to some shepherd, *unless* the sense of man's imperfection is loosed from the drive for endings. Perhaps what is needed is a sense of no ending, of the unending, but not as the dialectical opposite of end or perfection.

We need images of the never-ending as much as those of goals and purposes and ends. Images of the interminable that we experience are as crucial as images for termination. Imperfection will have no sense of its own until it can be released from Greek philosophical and Christian theological ideas of ending, which is like saying, until the shepherd is freed from his obligation to the ones whom he thinks of as black or lost sheep, and until those feeling sheepish are liberated in that sense from the protective custody of some one they imagine to be a good shepherd.

It is by no means simple, this quest for imperfection's sense. It is not simple precisely because the task may itself be construed as a search for yet another end, becoming thereby another perfection to be achieved. All our nurture—in education, religion, life—has taught us to look for the end, the ending, not realizing that our manner of looking was itself binding us to *impossible* perfectionism, imitating this shepherd or that, sheepishly seeking protection and love, then wondering why we felt fleeced, lost, or slaughtered. An entire Western tradition taught us the way, imagined it for us. We do not easily change this course.

Yet that is what is required. What is required is to sense imperfection in a way different from perfection's sense, to imagine the "no end" in a way radically unlike imagining ends and endings, whether tragic or comic, religious or secular, social or psychological. One can almost sense that there may be no end to this matter, this imagining "no ending." Yet it would be a different "no end" from the circular, double-binding endlessness of perfection's tasks. At the end of perfection's endlessness one begins to feel the "no end" of imperfection. Yet one still has no sense of it, no image, no way of imagining. This is just the problem: lack of imagination.

We need a way of sensing at last, without coming to the end of the matter, what Heraclitus meant when he said: "You can never find the end of soul, even if you travelled every road, such is the depth of its meaning."[5]

Imagine knowing this, yet not knowing how to get a sense for it; knowing it as an imperfection, yet not having an image of it. Imagine that: not being able to image. Not being able to end . . . nor not to end, either. Not perfect. Imperfect. No end to it. No end . . .

5 JESUS, THE MODEL OF IMPERFECTION

PERHAPS a review is in order. It all began with the sense of an obligation to be perfect, though already at the outset there was an intuition of perfection's impossibility. Then we noted a powerful image lying hidden in perfection's sense, an archetypal form. It was a double image: the figure of the Good Shepherd and his Sheep. As reflection continued, implications were found in all aspects of life, in social relationships and psychological meaning, in religion and secular imagination, in our every understanding.

Then it turned. Something moved in the understanding when thought was given to the "end" of it, when it was observed how being sheep or shepherd perfectly seemed to have no end and yet was at the same time bound and committed to some end. So a new need was sensed, a need for images of imperfection released from perfection's sense, an archetypal image of "no end," a different theological imagination, another christology for our soul. The task shifted. An aphorism by Franz Kafka catches it: "What is laid upon us is to accomplish the negative; the positive is already given." [1]

Kant attempted a similar thing in philosophy when he tried to release aesthetics from the idea of "end." The principle location of this work is the book *Critique of Judgment*. The argument is complex, but Martin Foss reviews it succinctly. "It was the great deed of Kant," Foss observes, "to eliminate the concept of perfection from aesthetics . . . he challenged the idea of 'end' in art. . . . The beautiful has nothing to do with any conceptual entity, therefore is not concerned with the concept of purpose and the conformity to purpose which is perfection. But Kant went still further . . . in the second aesthetic entity, the SUB-LIME. He discovered a sphere which is repulsion, a destruction and violation of end and perfection, a total negation of these values. Here is the culminating point of this new aesthetics: that which is inexpedient, inadequate, a negation to end and purpose, that which in the highest degree is imperfect . . . , the challenge to perfection and satisfaction, is aesthetically sublime." [2]

C. G. Jung has mounted a psychological argument not unlike Kant's philosophical one and the present theological one. He first noted the psychological impact on an individual of the pervasive, even if unconscious, theological definition of "evil" as *privatio boni* ("the privation of good"). Such an idea depends upon a prior notion of what is "good" (*boni*). It also implies that God or the Ideal or Being is all-good and that evil is not a thing-in-itself but is rather only the human or real or historical falling short of what is good. But this does not conform to our experience, psychologically, which sometimes seems to present the ideal and the real as mixed together and sometimes seems to manifest shadow-experiences which are objective and transpersonal, not being privations of anything good. So Jung concludes, as a therapist, that the actual function of *privatio boni* is to produce too much optimism concerning "evil" (it is merely a privation of good) and too much pessimism concerning the self (it is my fault). Jung therefore attempts to articulate a psychology that will be released from the implicit perfectionist obligation of this theology.[3]

It would be a relatively simple matter to nominate rival images to those of perfection, replacing theology with secular technology, with social or political programs, or with psychological therapy; or, replacing the image of the shepherd with those of, say, farmers, sailors, or warriors; or, replacing christology with guruism, piety with politics, West with East, hard purposeful work with purposeless play, and so on.[4] But it is not without good reason that Jung, commenting on the shepherd dream of a client (an "animus woman," he calls her), said that though the land of the sheep in the dream is an image of childish egoism desiring protection, "it is just as childish to move away and then assume that childhood no longer exists because we do not see it."[5] Jung rather prescribes that the "conscious mind suffer itself to be led back" to the land of the sheep, but in a new way.

Shepherd and sheep, our perfectionist sense with its double-binding obligation, and our dedication to ends are simply *there* to be reckoned with in life-experience. They will not go away by probing imperfection's substitutions. Jewish tradition, Christian orthodoxy, and the reticence of the people's slang have resisted the shepherd's perfectionism. Yet the sense persists. Why?

The achievement of the negative in life will not be under way radically until we are able to discover the sense of imperfection *within* the very archetypal figure that haunts and binds perfection's impossibility. Only in such a way may one find a real sense of imperfection released from one more of perfectionism's obligations.

The proposal is not to flee theology or its images, substituting something for it or inventing some new fad. The suggestion rather is to work one's way into it more deeply, exploring the mythology behind it, locating the anatomy of its imaginal world, and then translating and transposing its mythic figures, the gods and goddesses, out of their hidden mythopoetic contexts into likenesses with lived experience.[6]

In the particular case of the sense of perfection and its related christological images, the Good Shepherd and the sheep, the task involves releasing sheep from shepherd without ignoring the autonomous power that each side of this complex has over life.[7] This will be a bit awkward, to be sure, since it means attempting to view Jesus the Shepherd as a model of *im*perfection![8] But then Kafka had said, "What is laid upon us is to accomplish the negative"—the imperfection of the Good Shepherd, a christopoesis of imperfection's sense of no end.

6 CHRIST THE LAMB AND HERMES THE RAM

CONNECTING pagan mythology with Christian theology, discovering the mythic tales of the gods in religious ideas, was a work already begun by the Church Fathers. But it is a work which in the main is ignored in our time. For example, early Christian preachers and thinkers linked Jesus' life and work to Prometheus, Herakles, Apollo, Asklepios, Odysseus . . . and this only begins to name the correspondences they saw. And yet, the particular task of mythologizing the christology of the Good Shepherd has no classical instance. Hermes, however, is an obvious candidate since, as we shall see, this Greek god, like Christ much later, was identified as both Shepherd and Sheep.[1]

The Jesuit theologian Hugo Rahner probed the Hermes/ Christ connection in an essay originally written for a book in honor of C. G. Jung. But Rahner made no mention of the images of shepherd or sheep.[2] Rather, he demonstrated how often the Church Fathers used the mythology of Hermes to make a point concerning Christ's function for mankind: both of them were "soul guides" (*psychogogoi*). Rahner particularly stressed, as did the Fathers, Hermes' spiritual role in saving man from the passions of the flesh. The common allusion is to *The Odyssey*, by Homer, where in Book Ten Hermes provides Odysseus with the tranquilizing drug, "moly," which will save the hero from the fleshly wiles of the seductive Circe and her women. For this material, Rahner relies especially on Justin's *Apology*, the pseudo-Clementine *Recognitiones*, and Hippolytus' *Elenchos*.[3]

But Rahner misses the opportunity to link Christ to Hermes by way of the shepherd-motif. The Fathers are similarly silent, and suspiciously so, even though Hippolytus did favor setting the date for Christmas on the second of April, which would have placed Jesus' birth appropriately, as the Church Father argues, under the sign of Aries the Ram.[4] Rahner's omission is all the more suspect in that he cites in his essay a lecture given by Karl Kerényi in which the latter stressed the notion of Hermes Kriophoros, "Hermes the Ram-bearer," a motif which is precisely a prototype, six centuries earlier, for the Christian iconography of Christ the Lamb-bearer.[5]

Kerényi recounted Pausanius' account of a festival at Tanagra where a youth, imitating the god Hermes, carried a ram on his shoulders while circumambulating the city walls.[6] Imhoof-Blumer and Gardner, in their work, *Numismatic Commentary on Pausanius*, have displayed sixth-century Greek coins carrying the imprint of Hermes shouldering the sheep.[7] Why did the Fathers, who surely knew this data, and Rahner, who had read Kerényi's work, refuse this obvious connection and focus instead entirely on the incident of the moly-drug?

Perhaps Pausanius' account is itself a clue to this problem. This ancient writer is strangely repressive in his report. He is telling about the Kaberoi Mysteries at Samothrace, how Saos, the founder of the island, was born from the union of Rhene the Queen and Hermes. Since the word *rhene* means "sheep," Hermes doubtless performed this act as a ram.[8] The ritual celebrating the occasion, which Pausanius himself observed, was apparently quite odd. About it, Pausanius says: "As for the story of Hermes and the ram told during the mystery . . . , I know it but will not tell it."[9] What is suspect about this is that it is so atypical of Pausanius, who customarily will disclose everything, even with considerable relish.

An account of the same event by the Christian, Clement of Alexandria, may bring us closer to the suspicion about Rahner's silence. Clement gives his account while inveighing against the extreme and disgusting obscenity of pagan mythology.[10] E. R. Goodenough, without sharing Clement's moralizing judgment, makes a similar observation, while listing Hermes' connection to sheep under the heading, "Symbols Primarily Erotic."[11]

Amon of Thebes, the Egyptian god taking the form of a sheep, has a similar erotic quality, as is indicated by two invocations to him: "Thou art the phallus of the master of the gods!" and "Thou art the living sheep, the primordial principle of virility, first of all the gods!"[12]

The same sexual tone is supported by the Greek association of Hermes' sheep and the honey of Dionysos. In Jewish iconography this becomes a mythological reference for the fertility of the promised land flowing with milk and honey. That is to say: the place hoped for is that of Hermes and Dionysos. So it is that a wall painting in Pompeii depicts two sheep pulling a chariot usually associated with Dionysos but which, in this case, actually contain the caduceus of Hermes. This wand is shown alongside wings, snakes, and a large leering satyr-mask.[13]

The Church Fathers were not reticent to link Hermes and Christ by referring to the *Logos,* Christ being the "Word" (*logos*) of God and Hermes being the messenger of the gods (their *logoi*). Clement of Alexandria connects such a christology to the image of the shepherd by saying: "Lead us, holy Shepherd of *rational* sheep . . . Thou Logos."[14] The idea here is hardly erotic, but is rather a rationalizing of shepherd and sheep, drawing the images into a perspective of the *logos*-logic of solar-moral-consciousness. This is also indicated by the writings of Philo, who identifies the shepherd as *nous*, the "intellectual principle" of life which shepherds the irrational and erotic powers of soul, helping man to act morally.[15]

Perhaps, then, the reason for the reticence of Rahner and the Fathers has to do with an inability to reconcile sexual imperfections with moral perfection in the stories of Hermes. To connect Hermes Kriophoros of Samothrace and Tanagra with Jesus Christophoros ("the Christopher") would involve an implication of a real carnality in the incarnation. Indeed, when Hermes is taken out of Homer's heroic and epic contexts, he not only does not save man from Circe's passion, but he himself participates in it fully! And what of Christ the Lamb? If theology could be released from the contexts of moral imitation and perfectibility, from monotheistic literalism and rational fundamentalism, that is, if the imaginal function of the Good Shepherd could be freed from a perfectionist theology, then perhaps a hermetic ram christology could suggest a new and more radical soul-sense.

A second motif in the stories of Hermes confirms this intuition. Phrixos was the son of Nephele and Athamas. This latter, in turn, was descended from the fated line of Prometheus, Deucalion, Aeolus, Sisyphus, and Ixion—each of whom suffered dreadfully for attempting to bring the secrets of the gods to man's immediate benefit.[16] Because of Hera's jealous wrath over some sexual matter, an oracle was sent to Athamas, a message that was perhaps purposely misinterpreted, saying that the gods required Athamas to sacrifice his son in order to show his faith in the deities. In despair, yet in full faith, the father led his son, Phrixos, to the top of a mountain and laid his son on the altar he had prepared. At the point of the killing, Herakles the hero attempted, but failed in his heroism, to wrest the knife from the father. Then Hermes interceded. He placed a ram in a bush nearby, or perhaps he was himself the ram.[17] Phrixos, on the ram's back, was flown East to the land of Colchis, from which place the ram's fleece was brought back to Greece by the hero, Jason, in another story.[18]

It goes without saying that the connection of this story to that of Abraham and Isaac is striking in the extreme. And insofar as the Hebrew story is the prototype for God's sacrifice of his Son for man, together with that Son's rescue, the connection of Hermes and Christ is again seen to be made through the motif of a ram.[19]

What may be most important, however, is Hermes' route with the solar-golden-fleeced animal. It is West to East rather than East to West, as is Jason's heroic achievement. It is a solar journey, to be sure, but it is not the daylight way. The secret of the golden ram is that the journey has to do with a nocturnal sun, a dark light, *sol niger,* as the alchemists called it. Hermes takes Phrixos under the world, the underworld route, the way of dying, a sacrifice of ego's daylight perspectives. Salvation in this instance is not *from* death, but *in* a dying.[20] A christology connecting to Hermes may reveal more than can meet the Church's solar theological eye!

If the Kabeiroi and Phrixos stories complicate a hermetic christology in a way not intended by orthodox interpretations, it is nonetheless a meaning that the mythological interpretations of the Fathers carries unconsciously and willy nilly as soon as Hermes is invoked as a figuration of Christ. Hermes corroborates, not our sense of perfection (hardly!), but some other sensuality, a sense which cannot forever avoid Circe by using a theological tranquilizer. It may involve one in a coupling with seductive Rhene.

This sensual image of the sheep reminds one more of Picasso's goats than all of the animals in the orthodox art of Byzantium. Indeed, by way of this hermetic ram, one may begin to understand Jung's saying about the Apocalypse of St. John: "The Lamb, transformed into a demonic ram, reveals a new gospel, the *Evangelium Aeternum.*"[21]

It is not a changing of sheep to goat, of positive to negative, of perfect to some opposite that still depends upon a perfectionist sense. It is rather the experience of the "divine-demonic ambiguity" (Tillich).[22] Sheep is seen, not to become, but to belong to the ram, configuring no longer with shepherd. The sheep/shepherd archetype, by way of Hermes, is reconstellated, releasing the innocent, imitative lamb from her status in the one flock of whatever shepherd, now finding another place, one with the ram, a place which it is the soul-task of every Psyche to confront, as Apuleius' tale of Eros and Psyche has shown.

But this raises a serious question. If the shepherd loses his sheep to the ram, he will have nothing to shoulder! What will then become of the shepherd's sense of vocation and of self, of his sense of identity *as* shepherd who herds sheep? How will he now be able to understand his shepherdness? Who is the Good Shepherd—really?

7 CHRIST THE SHEPHERD AND THE MONSTER CYCLOPS

THERE are many archetypal images of the shepherd in the mythologies of the world, many models for identifying the Good Shepherd. For example, there are the Sumerian, Dumuzi; the Egyptian, Amon; the Greeks, Pan, Orpheus, Paris, and Apollo, this last having worked the sheepfolds of King Admetus; the Tibetan, Avalokiteshwara, who is incarnate in the Dalai Lama; the Hindu, Krishna, an avatar of Vishnu; and even the magician, Merlin, who is seen as a shepherd in the mode of Merlinus Sylvester.[1] But in a context of the problems surrounding perfectionism—a context of the single-eyed traditions of Oneida and Ranter communities,[2] and of Hermas' saying that a perfect faith has no double-mindedness[3]—the figure of the shepherd which comes forcefully to mind is the monster cyclops, Polyphemos,[4] who, like the South Asian god Shiva, has a great eye in the middle of his forehead.[5] Homer tells the story.

On the way home from the war, just before wrestling with

Circe's seduction, Odysseus confronts a different passion. Polyphemos, king of the Cyclopes, is described as Odysseus' problem. This cyclops is "gigantic," a "lout," "having a single eye," "lacking in law," "deciding justice for himself," "living in a wilderness," "in a cavern," "knowing none but savage ways," "a brute," "huge," "like a shaggy mountain," "wild," "ignorant of civility," "not believing in the gods," "mad," "unbearable," and "a bloody monster." [6]

Odysseus' error is one typical of heroic man. He stays on, having stolen the cheese and meat he came for, curious to see the monster. This is a mistake because Polyphemos is cannibalistic. The heroic man is engulfed by his appetites. So Odysseus becomes trapped in the cave of the monster. Being of some wit and trickery, however, he plots how to escape the cyclopic fate, this deep cavern and the gaze of the wild eye.

Using some of the wine of Apollo which he had received earlier from Maron, Odysseus makes the giant drunk. As Polyphemos sleeps off the potent drink, the heroes hew the end of an olive tree which the Cyclops uses as a shepherd's staff, heating it red hot in the fire, and

> . . . bored that great eye socket
> While blood ran out around the red hot bar.
> Eyelid and lash were seared; the pierced ball
> Hissed broiling, and the roots popped. [7]

The homeric author likens the scene to that of a smithy, where hot metal is plunged into a cold bath, "just so, that eyeball hissed around the spike."

When the monster, screaming in agony, asked the name of the one responsible for this terrible deed, Odysseus lied and said his name was "Nobody." So the giant, asking for help from the other cyclopes, said, "Nobody has hurt me." The others therefore assumed he had no need.

It remained only for Odysseus to escape the deep cave. The Cyclops had covered the entrance with a slab of rock. But in his desperation, Polyphemos threw away the stone and sat in his own doorway in order to catch the culprit should he attempt to flee. The monster shepherd thereby became the door of his own sheepfold, like Christ in the Fourth Gospel. Nonetheless, Odysseus avoided the now-blinded monster by binding his men and himself to the sheep, becoming, as it were, themselves like these animals. In this way, they passed to pasture in safety with the coming of the next morning's dawn.

Only when safely out of the range of Polyphemos' grasp did the hero curse the blinded giant in a loud voice, at the same time revealing his own true name. It was then that the monster "saw" for the first time the real meaning of Telemos' prophecy about his future fate. He had not been suspicious of this heroic mortal because, as he said,

> *Always I had in mind some giant, armed*
> *In giant force, would come against me here.*
> *But this, but you—small, pitiful and twiggy—*
> *You put me down with wine, you blinded me.*[8]

From this perspective the heroic is small, and the monster with the single eye sees truly only when he is blinded, that is, when seeing from the cavern of his voided head.[9] Cycloptic vision is cave-vision. The word, "cyclops," literally means "circle eyed." There is no circle round the eye till some burning pike puts it out, till it is blackened, darkened, till there are rings under the eyes, wrinkles. Then the seeing of the "nobody" of heroism from the nothingness of the cave becomes one with prophetic vision. The vision comes from the wounded eye, single-vision's hurt. It is a grotesque story, to be sure. It has to do with the suffering of the putting out of perfection's perspective, the eye of the shepherd who is experienced as monstrous.[10] So goes the epic tale of Homer.

Euripides tells a different story. This poet's time, perhaps not too unlike our own, saw traditional religious mythology differently, if indeed it could be seen at all in an age when gods were dead or dying. Meanings were no longer available to the people in epic proportion, in homeric version, in olympic grandeur.

The poet's task in a time of dearth involves a re-mythologizing.[11] Therefore, Euripides wrote no epic poem. He wrote a drama called *The Cyclops*, and it was a satyr-play.

The differences are these. (1) Being a satyr-tale, no longer epic, the myth takes on a different tone, yet without losing its grotesque sense. Now it is humorous, and often ironically so. (2) It thereby connects the story, not to such as Athena and Zeus, but to Silenos and Dionysos, and in the latter case more to the comic than to the tragic face.[12] (3) Polyphemos and Silenos not only drink together; they also are male lovers. Polyphemos, in all this, is a sort of "lovable buffoon," [13] and Silenos is prototypically a lewd, bald, fat, boastful, knavish, drunken Falstaff. (4) Most important, however, is the fact that in Euripides' version of the story there never was a stone in front of the Cyclops' cave. Escape was possible all the while. The heroism of blinding the monster, putting out his vision, was unmotivated. The barbarism and ugliness of the act, ironically, implicates the hero as the true monster. The little man who is civilized is the real barbarian. Roles are reversed. Sympathies shift dramatically.

A little while later in Greek history, Theocritus continued this irony by making Polyphemos not only a lovable buffoon but even a lover. In a romantic *Idyll*, the poet pictures the monster, like the Good Shepherd of John's Gospel, as referring to himself as *kalos*, "good" or "beautiful." Polyphemos the Shepherd proclaims his love for a resistant Galatea. He says: "A thousand sheep I feed." [14] Thus, not only is the hero now the monster, but *the monster is the true shepherd*. It is he who is faithful to us. What we, like Galatea, not to mention the heroic Odysseus, perceive to be grotesque and ugly in the deep cavern of some island haunt, is that which really loves us deeply, that whose fidelity we can really trust.

This perspective is a vision not outside Plato's cave in the rational sun-lit mind, but is one within that of Polyphemos. It is, as El Gallo says in the musical drama *The Fantasticks*, that "without a hurt the heart is hollow." The hollowness, as the

Cyclops found, is a way of seeing. So El Gallo instructs the audience:

> ... *try to see it,*
> *Not with your eyes, for they are wise;*
> *But see it with your ears;*
> . . . .
> *And hear it with the inside of your hand.*[15]

Heraclitus had already said it: "Eyes . . . are bad witnesses to men having barbarian souls." [16]

There is a similar cycloptic suggestion in Joyce Cary's novel *The Horse's Mouth,* where the freakish artist, Gulley Jimson, instructs his mistress on how to look at a painting, saying, "Don't look at it. Feel it with your eye." [17] Such insightful feeling by way of cycloptic vision may accompany an experience of the violence of "nobody" putting out external vision, depriving one of images merely visual, of imagination which requires external literalization.

When the gods of a heroic theology are eclipsed, archetypal patterns of myth still function, but no longer in a literal way, being no longer moralistic guides for imitative behavior. How the mythology works in such times is suggested by the fact that the cyclopes were, as Roscher notes, *Gewitterdämonen,* "storm(y) spirits." [18] They were constantly being cast into the underworld of Tartaros by first this and then that olympic deity. That they are "storm gods" may be connected with imagining them as having a single eye. It may be linked with the vortex or void at the center of a storm. We speak, for example, of the "eye" of a cyclone or hurricane. The suggestion of this imaginal association is that cycloptic vision comes from the soul's storm, like Job's vision out of the whirlwind of suffering.[19]

Mythology's meaning is seen out of soul's storm, as in the case of dreams, where myths are indeed present, but, as in the instance of Euripides, now displaced, disfigured, condensed, censored, distorted, deformed, reassembled in bits and pieces, or under the influence of humor or wit-work. No longer is it mythology; it is now mythopoesis.

A christopoesis that views *the Good Shepherd as a monster in everyday life-experience* (Chapter III, above) may, through the transforming satyr-vision of Euripides and Theocritus, begin to see *the deep monsters of soul's storms as shepherding.* Some points of connection begin to appear.

1. There is the suggestion of the Gospels, "if your eye causes you to sin, pluck it out" (Matthew 18:9a; Mark 9:47a), and St. Paul's identification of the revelation which comes "through the spirit" as being "what no eye has seen" (I Corinthians 2:9–10).[20]

2. The blinding of Polyphemos the Shepherd begins to give mythological background for John's placing the pericope of Christ the Good Shepherd in the context of Jesus' saying to the literalist Pharisees: "For judgment I came into this world, that those who do not see may see, and that those who see may become blind."[21] This theme of seeing in blindness stretches from Tiresias to St. Paul, and from Jesus, who was blindfolded by Roman soldiers and then asked to prophesy, to the children's game of Blind Man's Buff and the contemporary play by Harold Pinter, *The Birthday Party.*[22]

3. We have already noted the correspondence between Polyphemos and Jesus as both being viewed as doors to the sheepfold, to the shepherd's cave. The suggestion is that these figures are entrances to a deep way of seeing out of a perspective of ego-blindness: a seeing from the perspective of imperfection![23]

There is yet one more step in these connections. Ovid tells of an old tradition in which the cyclopes were originally smiths, their third eye, like that of Shiva, not to mention the Buddha, representing the igniting fire of the forge (*agni*).[24] They were the armor-makers for Zeus until Apollo reduced them to shepherd-status in a dispute over Asklepios' ability to eliminate death, depriving Hades of his part in the nature of things.[25]

Apollo's perfectionism conceals the true nature of these shepherds: they work the forge! This is to say, behind the one who cares for the animal—whether shepherd, pastor, teacher, friend, parent, or therapist—there lurks one who forges metal, some smith or perhaps an alchemist.

Studies in the history of religions and comparative mythology confirm this connection between Shepherd and Smith. For example, the mythology of Cain and Abel bears testimony to it. The name, "Cain" (Arabic *gayin* and Aramaic *gena'ā*), and the vocation of the tribes of Kenites (that is, "Cain-ites"), indicate a pariah status for smiths in pastoral societies. Smiths are indeed outcasts in certain tribes of Africa, Arabia, Iran, India, and Nepal. The name of Cain's brother, "Abel," means "herdsman" (Syriac *habla*, Arabic *ibl,* and Akadian *ibilu*).[26] It is noteworthy in this regard, also, to recall those warring brothers, Atreus and Thyestes, whose sibling strife in ancient Greece produced a notable curse on the house of Atreus which culminated in the Oresteian tragedy. Their original battle was a fight over a gold *ram!*

The story of Cain connects with the Cyclops mythology, not only in its shepherd and warring motifs, but also by way of its cannibalism. In the *Clementine Homily,* the giants who were born of the union of the angels and the daughters of Cain were devourers of human flesh, like Polyphemos.[27] But this is still not the end.

Mircea Eliade reports the common link between smith and shaman by way of a Yakut proverb: "Smiths and shamans are from the same nest."[28] So it is that the origin of our word "blacksmith" has to do with "black magic," that is, the magic performed by the shaman who was later to become a shepherd.

The mark of Cain—common in many tribes—is the mark of one who works the forge. It is a mark in the middle of the forehead, not as a punishment for moral disobedience, but as signifying the fire (remember *agni,* "ignite") of the forge. It is like the solar eye of the Cyclops, but blackened by occupation, hence, *sol niger,* "the black sun." [29] Can it then be accidental that a common initiation of the Siberian shaman included the tearing out of the eyes of the initiate?!

The point of all this for a cyclopic christology is that it joins the Johannine Good Shepherd to a hunting/fishing milieu rather than to an agrarian/pastoral tradition.[30] The philosophers Plato and Aristotle, who laid the ideological base for the agrarian-rooted civilization of the West, both utilized the image of the Cyclops as the *enemy* of culture, a veritable mythic prototype of civilization's discontented ones.[31] So to understand one's self and one's world as civilized, from this point of view, it is necessary to repress that which is grotesque, freakish, and monstrous. That is, the benefits of culture are purchased at the cost of a sense of imperfection's function in life.

Thus, a cycloptic christology would not be one of growth (agrarian and pastoral), yielding fruits of perfection, but rather of hunt, where the animal is not domesticated but is befriended, precisely for the purpose of killing, a monstrous act, grotesque in the extreme, to be sure, but part of life. Such a view asks: "Am I my brother's keeper?" It implies in the very question some remarkable alchemy of the wounded animal-soul. It is something that is deeper and more primitive than metaphors of growing (agriculture) and herding (shepherds and sheep) which have been so pervasive to the Western theological and secular imagination. It takes account of another side of life, symbolized by a radical reading of the Mass, for example: not man eating Christ, but the shepherd devouring the sheep. When the gigantic monster devours the human, the human becomes primordially gigantic: transpersonal, archetypal. Behind the shepherd who eats the flock is a smith who slaughters the shepherd. Cain is to Abel as Polyphemos is to human heroism odysseying its way through life.

If the shepherd in everyman could realize deep within himself a monstrous blacksmith or a blind ogre who sees shamanistically, this new configuration might release the sheep to mate once again with the ram, rather than being forever wed to some shepherd. In such a remythologizing, a christology of the shepherd might become a source for our sense of imperfections, as it has been a source of perfectionism. Polyphemos, too, is a Good Shepherd.

It goes without saying that some will shy from this sort of christopoesis. They will say, with academic or pietistic horror, that attempts to connect Christ and the Cyclops are grotesque, fanciful, allegorist, and imperfect. Such persons could invoke the sacred theological dictum of Tertullian which says that Athens has nothing to do with Jerusalem, mythology is irrelevant to Christian theology. They could even insist that New Testament meanings must finally be grounded in Hebrew tradition, not Greek, and that surely no cycloptic themes are to be found in Jewish backgrounds to Christianity. This reticence, however, can be met directly.

In the second dream-vision of the Book of Enoch, Israel's entire history is cast in terms of the metaphors of shepherding. We are told that the Lord of the Sheep has a face "terrible to behold," a description with stunning parallel to Homer's account of Polyphemos. But further, the motif of the blinding of the shepherd, is a litany throughout.[32] Yet even this is not the most striking instance of the cycloptic theme.

We have already referred to a passage in the prophecy of Zechariah which one interpreter called the "most enigmatic in the Bible." [33] What is enigmatic is that the shepherd is God, and God, strange to say, monstrously devours the sheep, like some cannibal. Then the text goes on to say that the shepherd himself is struck down, saying, in remarkable language: "Let . . . his right eye (be) utterly blinded" (Zechariah 11.17). What is perhaps most surprising of all is that no Biblical scholar has made the connection to the story of Polyphemos, an association that would certainly make less "enigmatic" this passage, since it connects Christ the Shepherd, by way of the messianic prophecy, with doors, slaughtering, prophetic abilities, blinding, and passion, but also with the Jewish reticence concerning shepherds and the orthodox theological difficulty with obligations to the impossible good works of perfection. So much comes together.

Jung once said, "There are more things in the Bible than theologians can admit," [34] suggesting by this that there might be something to the saying of St. Paul, "The foolishness of God is wiser than men." [35] Erasmus, who is well known for his praise of the folly of God, also wrote, in 1529, on the subject of "Cyclops, the Gospel Bearer." In this dialogue, Cannius asks: "By Herakles! What has Polyphemos to do with the Gospels?" And Polyphemos replies: "You might as well ask what a Christian has to do with Christ!" [36]

8 SHEPHERD AND CLOWN

THERE remains a problem. It is well and good to imagine a reconfiguration of the theological complex of shepherd and sheep, remythologizing it into a hermetic and cycloptic christology. But are Hermes and Polyphemos really any more immediate to us than Jesus? Can a mythology that is archaic provide us with imperfection's sense any more than a theology that is impossibly perfectionistic?

Not only Euripides but also Rudolf Bultmann, Jung as well as Freud, all knew that without myth we are nothing, but that myth often seems unavailable to modernity's experience of felt-mythlessness. Euripides' strategy with the myth of Polyphemos is an instance of his agonizing over this issue, repoetizing the mythology precisely out of the deprivation of myth, out of the cycloptic vortex, the void, the nothingness. His Polyphemos shows, not only the dark of solar consciousness, not only the archetypal ground of psychology's ego-concept, not only the polytheistic base of monotheistic religion, but also a present poesis, a poetizing of meaning. His satyr play demonstrates the task involved in the poetry of religion's mythology: theopoetic.

Euripides' strategy is to find a *third*, some "other" to which Cyclops and Odysseus are both related and in whom their relationship to each other is expressed. But it must be a "third" to whom we can all readily relate. Euripides names Silenos the Satyr, the Clown, the Fool.

Silenos may well play an important implicit role, like he does in Euripides' mythopoesis, in a hermetic and cycloptic christology. In splitting the shepherd/sheep archetype, discovering the ram to which the sheep truly belongs in a complex of Hermes, and finding the blacksmith with whom the monstrous shepherd, Polyphemos, is at home, opens the possibility, as was implied at the very end of the last chapter, of sensing the "foolishness" of religious meaning. Perhaps, indeed, Silenos can teach us the *present* significance of Hermes and Polyphemos as archetypal christic images, since, in some sense we surely know the "clown." [1]

The clown manifests Hermes. Like the hermetic ram of Samothrace, the clown is physical, bodily, sensuous, and obscene. His accouterments are asses ears, cockscomb, leatherstocking phallus, tongue bladder, and slapstick. These correspond to Hermes' herm, the eternally erect phallus which leads this guide of souls to Hades' deeper realm, finding "holes" in the earth, doors to the "other," "under" worlds. The clown's sensual physicality is well-known by the imperfections of his falls, the fall on the prat, a pratfall, as it is called. The word "fool" (Latin *follis*) suggests "scrotum," as the Italian *coglione* for "dolt" literally means "testicles." [2] All this belongs to Hermes' domain.

But the clown also manifests the Cyclops. His figure is well-known as grotesque, monstrous, and freakish. The first court fool, so far as anyone knows, was a pygmy presiding at the court of Dadkeri-Assi, Pharoah in Egypt's Fifth Dynasty.[3] More than 2000 years later, Cortez discovered freaks and grotesques functioning as fools in the Aztec court of Montezuma II.[4]

The place of the freak and madman in the entire history of the fool and clown is well-known to historians and, for that matter, to any who frequent circuses. But there is more to link clown to Cyclops than just the grotesque.

Willeford, in speaking of the ability of the clown to sense imperfection's primacy without depending on perfection's obligation, notes a strange paradox—and here he is speaking primarily of Shakespeare's fools: "Of course, *seeing through* illusions and even *through* the conventional structures that make understanding possible may be expressed as *not seeing at all.* The latter may, in fact, be a symptom or even a precondition of the former—as in the familiar figure of the wise man as blind seer." [5] Polyphemos' understanding of Telemos' prophecy after being blinded is an instance of this, as was noted in the last chapter. Another instance is that of the American comedian, Red Skelton, who said, after years of suffering pratfalls on the stage, "I've got the sixth sense, but I don't have the other five!" [6]

We certainly would not want to lose touch with the clown's sense, the soul's fool, the humor, for his slapstick is our imaginal access to Hermes' ram and his grotesque freakishness carries for us Polyphemos' blind "vision." Nor will the clown desert us, though *we* may lose the sense of him and of his strange cyclopic/hermetic humor. When the clown seems to die, as in the nineteenth and twentieth centuries, we can be assured that it will take yet another fool to perform his odd funeral, as Frederico Fellini's film *The Clowns* showed. The fool, it seems, reappears in his own dying, for the death of the fool, whether in self or society, would be itself grotesque, which is to say, it would be yet another piece of foolishness.

Perhaps, then, just as our christology may need the mythology of Hermes and the Cyclops, so it may also need the clown to bring body and soul to a hermetic/cycloptic christology.

Without the clown's sense our Gospel may be docetically spiritualist and aristotelianly intellectualistic. Yet great care must be taken at this very point, lest instead of achieving a repoetizing of the mythic background to a theological theme, bringing it nearer to our lives, we may once again lose it all romantically, becoming aesthetic or nostalgic about the clown and his humor.

One safeguard against idealizing the clown is to note that, just as the Good Shepherd is a Fool, so the clown is just a shepherd. In fact, we might have been alert to the shepherd-clown connection when, some chapters back, there was mention of Shakespeare's Touchstone. This clown called to the shepherd, Corin, saying: "Holla, you clown," thereby identifying the pastoral convention in poetry (see pages 11ff, above) with the history of the fool.[7]

There is an ancient Greek background to the Shakespearean association of shepherd and clown. In classical tragedies the messenger bringing the news of monstrously tragic events, often grotesque murders that could not be acted out on stage, was typically a shepherd. This messenger was also represented as being a comic figure. There are notable instances of this in Euripides, as, for example, in *The Bacchae*.[8]

The English word, "clown," itself links fool and shepherd. The term *colonus* or *clod* originally indicated a "farmer," or "rustic," or "shepherd." There is this same connection played upon in the Second Wakefield Shepherd's play, where the shepherd plays comic fool to everything.

Cain and Abel are to this point, too, as is the farmer/shepherd warring brotherhood, generally (see pages 40ff, above). The history of the clown makes the association. Clowns often present themselves as twins, a warring pair, or what is called the *döppleganger* ("doubles"). This began in ancient Roman times with the twin "zani," but is well-known in literature and circus alike. There are: Lear and the Fool, Quixote and Sancho Panza, Don Giovanni and Leporello, Tom Sawyer and Huckleberry

Finn, Shem and Shaun, Laurel and Hardy, Tweedledum and Tweedledee, Abbott and Costello, Groucho and Chico, Auguste and Whiteface, Hope and Crosby, Graciosos and Bobo, Arlecchino and Pedrolino, Burns and Allen, Martin and Lewis, Rowan and Martin. One is typically witty, like Hermes, tall as a herm, a *straight* man; the other, gross as Polyphemos, beaten like this Cyclops, the butt.[9]

So the shepherd is a clown, and the clown shepherds our sense of imperfection with his humor, a humor never lacking in the strife known to warring brothers, in a feel for the monstrous and grotesque, in a comic vision that sees through tragic blindness, and in a down-to-earth physical sensuality. If we lose touch with such sense from time to time, our poets, the "antennae of the race," manage to remind us. It is through them that we may see what has happened to the shepherd/clown/monster in our life's time.

There is a rich clown-literature abroad. It may come nearer to a hermetic and cycloptic depth than the christology of contemporary theologians. The literary work—like the paintings by Rouault of clowns which so resemble his depictions of Christ in their blackened, disfigured style—lends shadows to the light of comic image so that a sense of reality is somehow achieved. There are, for example: Heinrich Böll's *The Clown; The Blacks,* by Jean Genet, which he subtitles, "A Clown Show"; Henry Miller's *The Smile at the Foot of the Ladder; The Comedians,* by Graham Greene; and Trevor Griffith's play called by the same name as Greene's novel; Kurt Vonnegut's odd work, *Slapstick,* dedicated to Laurel and Hardy; and, of course, the film of Fellini already mentioned. The clowns of these works, and many others like them, poetize mythic monsters and hermetic rams through their silenic fooling-around.

Yet the clownish figure in contemporary literature who most directly connects motifs of Hermes and the Cyclops to shepherding is Sir Henry Harcourt-Reilly, the psychiatrist, in

T. S. Eliot's play *The Cocktail Party*. He enters the drama in a manner loved by Hermes and in the way of so many monstrous shepherds, namely, as an "unidentified guest." We begin to see his mythic link to Silenos-Polyphemos and their shepherding when he sings:

> As I was drinkin' gin and water,
>   And me bein' the One Eyed Riley, . . .
> Tooryooly toory-iley
>   What's the matter with One Eyed Riley? [10]

In the play, this shepherding psychiatrist guides what is called a "blind journey," an "endless struggle," employing all the while a clowning "sense of humour." The therapy he performs, like the "no end" of imperfection, is referred to as "unfinished." It doesn't take Julia's comment about his being a "dreadful man" to alert us to his cycloptic nature. She says, not unlike Theocritus' Galatea: "I was afraid of him at first; / He looks so forbidding." [11]

Eliot's picturing of the cycloptic and hermetic psychiatrist revises for modern consciousness the sense of the Good Shepherd of the soul. This poet's contemporary imagination suggests a reformation of the tradition of pastoral literature referred to earlier. Indeed, One Eyed Riley's behavior hints at the end of the idyllic shepherd and the turn to a more monstrous one, one already lurking in the mythological background of Hermes and Polyphemos. What Eliot depicts as a modern sensibility—that is, that we are today somehow closer to Hermes and Polyphemos than to a prettified picture of the Good Shepherd—is confirmed in other literature.

Wallace Stevens, for example, writes about a "black shepherd." [12] Then, in a different poem, he makes the meaning of "black," when used with "shepherd," clearer:

> These are the voices of the pastors calling
> And calling like the long echoes in long sleep,

Generations of shepherds to generations of sheep.
Each truth is a sect though no bells ring for it.
And the bells belong to the sextons, after all,
As they jangle and dangle and kick their feet.[13]

It is as if the poet were saying that the pastoral image of the shepherd no longer has a "ring" for modern man. It has made "sheep" of us all. Now the "ring" of truth in religious meaning seems more to belong to the dance ("jangle and dangle and kick their feet") of the common people ("sexton"). Meanwhile, the image of the pastoral shepherd has gone underground, as it were, functioning unconsciously in ways we might little suspect. Such is Stevens' suggestion in these lines:

As it was,
A dead shepherd brought tremendous
chords from hell
And bade the sheep carouse.[14]

This talk about sheep carousing and the shepherd being dead is certainly a far distance from the Gospel of John, and yet it sounds strikingly like the Hermes and Cyclops mythologies that we have identified as lying behind the motif of the Good Shepherd in the New Testament.

Already in classical times the shepherd's death was announced by a poet. In Aeschylus' play, *The Agamemnon*, there is a warning, given by the Chorus, concerning what will happen one day to a shepherd (Paris and the people of Troy) if there is an attempt to take care of the cute little baby animal (Helen). It may later turn out to have been, not a lamb at all, but a lion's cub which, when grown, will destroy the one who took it into caring arms. Shepherding, in this case, brings on a Trojan War.[15]

The underworld grotesqueness ("brought tremendous chords from hell") of the pastoral imagination in modern life is witnessed to also by James Dickey. He writes in one poem about "farm boys wild to couple / With anything" that produces a "thing that's only half / Sheep like a wooly baby / Pickled in alcohol."[16] Dickey here is writing from an impression he received while looking at a foetus preserved in a museum in Atlanta. This freakish experience is turned, by way of the poetic imagination, into a reflection on the monstrous products which follow from living out the life of the pastoral shepherd.

A similar mythopoetic strategy is used by the poet Robinson Jeffers to indicate what has become of the Christianized pastoral convention in human meaning. Jeffers wrote a letter to Sidney Alberts in which he confessed that "the loving shepherdess" in the poem of the same name was a figure designed to explore the "savior complex" in a long Christian culture.[17] The poet felt this complex "to be the most insidious and seductive syndrome to attack men of good will."[18]

In the poem, Jeffers' shepherdess is a pathetic California woman whose sensual passion and care lead not only to her own death but also to the loss of the sheep for which she cared. The loss of the herd was due not a little to her also attempting to shepherd the lusts of this cowboy, that outlaw, and so on. The horrifying poem ends with the shepherdess dying in labor while giving birth to the child of one who had raped her. The poem says:

> In the evening, between the rapid
> Summits of agony before exhaustion,
>   she called
> The sheep about her and percieved that
>   none came.[19]

Only those who are sheep respond to the call of the image of the shepherd, and there are none of those left! Surely these lines of Jeffers announce the end of the idyllic version of the pastoral mood.[20]

The writers depicting the sense of the shepherd in our time are implicating tones of the erotic-grotesque and the soul of the physical body in fantasies of protection and care. They seem to be suggesting that when we sense sheepish perfectionism in life, we might hope, not for a shepherd to take care of us, but for a ram with which to mate. When, on the other hand, we feel some sense of a shepherd's obligation, we might not demand lambs for a following, but search for the monster or smith in our own souls. For lurking in the circus of our interior ram and monster there may be a silenic clown taunting the ringmaster (the ego), a fool which is tutoring the court's king. That clodish clown, that comic fool, await our recognition, for in them we are reminded that the Good Shepherd has a monstrous shadow side, and yet his function is to put us in touch with what may be grotesque in the self and in the world, without being ourselves possessed by it unwittingly, as may indeed happen when one is overtaken by the gigantic duties of the Good Shepherd's perfectionism.

When it is sufficiently cycloptic and hermetic, the clown's vision, carrying the silenic connection, can give appropriate image to our sense of imperfection. This of course implies a new, or very old, "sense of self," as Wallace Stevens calls it, moving us, as this poet notes, "out of our lives to keep us in our death, / To watch us in the summer of Cyclops, Underground."[21]

There is no end to this underground, the depth of such imagination, the sensing of imperfection. Theodore Roethke calls it "infirmity," and mentions that it takes a special eye to see it, perhaps the one which comes when others are put out. Roethke writes:

> In purest song one plays the constant fool
> As changes shimmer in the inner eye.
> I stare and stare into a deepening pool
> . . . .
> The deep eye sees the shimmer on the stone.[22]

One begins to sense in the deepening pool of life no end to that shimmer, that stone. Imagine it: imperfection as a silenic shimmer on the rock of a hermetic/cycloptic Christ. A clown, perhaps, with a deep eye: a shimmer, a stone, and no end to it. Imperfect. No end . . .

PART TWO

CHRIST, THE CLOWN

9 CLOWN AND CHRIST

AT THE conclusion of Part One there came a somewhat unholy wedding of terms. Clown and Christ! To be sure, the connection made there was quite indirect. It proceeded by way of Silenos and his relation in Greek mythology to Hermes the Ram and to the Shepherd, Cyclops. Yet, however astonishing this justaposition of images may at first seem, the connection may well be more direct than has so far been indicated.

In fact, there is a growing twentieth-century literature, in academic theology and in secular fiction, which asserts a link between the figures of Christ and the clown. It is, as Harvard theologian Harvey Cox called it, "a new iconography of Christ." [1] Something is sensed; something, intuited. But what?

On the one side, there are theologians who want to show a religious or christic dimension to the experience of folly or to the figure of the clown. Yale theologian Jaraslov Pelikan wrote a work in this vein entitled *Fools for Christ*, this title being taken from a saying by St. Paul in I Corinthians 4:10. [2] Walter Nigg, a

European scholar, has written a work with a function similar to that of Pelikan's. Nigg draws upon Erasmus, Dostoievski, and Cervantes for his argument, one which is already revealed in his title, *Der christliche Narr* ("The Christ-like Fool").[3] An article by Lesek Kolakowski, entitled "The Priest and the Jester," [4] carries a similar theme, as does the book by Harvey Cox to which we have already alluded, though *The Feast of Fools* may belong to a second category of argument.

Cox's thinking is not as concerned to see the religious or christic nature of our experience of folly so much as it is attempting to view the person and work of Christ as in some important sense clownish or comedic. His phrase "Christ the Harlequin" means to release the Church's traditional theological images of Jesus from a certain over-seriousness. The point is to get some sense of dance and play back into religious piety: a real, physical sense of grace. Cox is by no means alone in this theological vocation.

Other works include the following: *The Humor of Christ* by Elton Trueblood,[5] *The Drama of Comedy: Victim and Victor* by Nelvin Vos,[6] *The Clown and the Crocodile* by Joseph McClelland,[7] *The Wit and Wisdom of Jesus* by George Buckley,[8] and *Holy Laughter* by Conrad Hyers.[9]

There is also a related work going on in New Testament studies, especially in the interpretation of the form typical of Jesus' preaching and teaching, namely, that of parables. The suggestion of these researches is that parables have an iconoclastic and comic function that may not be noticed by serious theologizing or by popular piety. Work by Robert Funk, Dan O. Via, and John Dominic Crossan are particularly notable in this regard,[10] as is an article by the European scholar, Geo Widengren, an article which links the conical hat of the whiteface clown to the garb of Western religious monks.[11]

This listing is by no means complete. It is given here simply to indicate that something is afoot amongst serious scholarship in theology, some intuition about the relation of Christ and clown. What that "something" is may well be suggested by a bit of verse which comes at the end of Cox's book.

> *Oh, we know our noses were itching for something*
> *With all the beads and mantras and incense.*

He is referring, of course, to the religious sensibility of the time as being deeply symptomatic of a profound need. Then Cox writes:

> *But he [Christ] was so gray and unavailable,*
> *Embalmed by church and state,*[12]

as if traditional theology was not helping in our time to meet the needs of soul, as if it were, by its "unavailable" intellectualistic modes, somehow depriving us of the carnality of the incarnation, of the real-life fleshly sense of christology. The implication is that imagining Christ as clown might bring some body to a sense of soul, some feeling to spiritual thought.

To be sure (as was mentioned in the last chapter), Picasso's art has shown the important physicality of the clown-figure, his crude, rude, obscene, gusty, freakish, grotesque, base reality. Rouault, too, was cited as picturing the implicit pain and suffering in the agonizing humor of the clown. But perhaps more to the point of the current theological literature on Christ and the clown are two contemporary novelists: Lawrence Durrell and Tom Robbins.

In the novel, *Clea,* the former writes:

> I was born under Jupiter, Hero of the Comic Mode! . . . I see art more and more clearly as a sort of manuring of the psyche. It has no intention, that is to say, no *theology*. By nourishing the psyche, by dunging it up, it helps to find its own level, like water. That level is an original innocence—who invented the perversion of Original Sin, that filthy obscenity of the West? . . . Why, for example, don't they recognize in Jesus the great Ironist that he is, the comedian? I am sure that two-thirds of the Beatitudes are jokes or squibs in the manner of Chuang Tzu. Generations of mystagogues and pedants have lost the sense.[13]

Tom Robbins, in a book called *Another Roadside Attraction,* manures the theological psyche in a similar way when he writes:

It delights us to watch a careless clown break taboos; it thrills us vicariously to watch him run wild and free; it reassures us to see him slapped down and order restored. . . . Consider Jesus as a ragged non-conforming clown—laughed at, persecuted and despised—playing out the dumb show of his crucifixion against the responsible pretensions of authority.[14]

Robbins continues by imagining for the reader a conversation between Jesus and Tarzan. The latter says that Jesus reminds him of the Greek god, Pan. Jesus asks why, and Tarzan replies:

There was a lot of love in that crazy rascal, just as there's a lot of love in you. . . . But he stunk, Pan did. In rutting season you could smell him a mile away. And he'd take on anything. He would've screwed this nanny goat if he couldn't find a nymph.[15]

Tarzan laughs at what he himself has just said. But Jesus, according to Robbins' text, doesn't "appreciate the references to carnal knowledge."[16]

The carnality of the incarnation; bringing religion down to earth: this seems to be the theme haunting both theological and secular interests in linking Christ to the clown. There is a stray metaphor in Harvey Cox's bit of verse that may be a clue to this theme. He mentions that "our *noses* were itching" (see also the comment by James Joyce in footnote #13, above). Strange as it may seem at first, it is precisely the *nose* upon which Wallace Stevens, also, focuses to make the point of the earthy reality of the comic figure. He is speaking about Crispin, to whom reference was made in passing at the end of the last chapter. The poem is called, "The Comedian as the Letter C." The relevant lines are these:

> . . . *A river bore*
> *The vessel inward. Tilting up his nose,*
> *He inhaled the rancid rosin, burly smells*
> *Of dampened lumber, emanations blown*
> *From warehouse doors, the gustiness of ropes,*
> *Decays of sacks, and all the arrant stinks*
> *That helped him round his rude aesthetic out.*[17]

The "comedian" journeys and quests, guided by his "nose." The trip is "inward," according to the poem, and it leads the "comedian," as later lines tell us, to prefer "text to gloss." He senses "rancid . . . burly smells," "gustiness," "decay," and "arrant stinks." His nose "helped him round his rude aesthetic out." As the poet says: "It made him see how much / Of what he saw he never saw at all." [18]

Cox and Stevens and Joyce are not the only ones concerned with noses. Friedrich Nietzsche, in 1875, wrote: "Our thinking should have a vigorous fragrance, like a wheatfield on a summer's night." Eighty-two years after Nietzsche's utterance, Martin Heidegger asked: "How many of us today still have the sense for that fragrance?" [19]

Alan Watts, for one, suspects we have lost the sense altogether. "We have no spectrum of smell, such as we have of light," he writes, and then continues:

A cat may look at a king, and I may listen with obvious attentiveness to what you are saying. I may sip your wine with overt gusto, and may even grasp your hand on meeting. . . . But quite deliberately to smell another person, unless she is your sweetheart, is beyond the pale and puts us in mind of dogs, snuffing at each other's bottoms. Aside from perfume on a woman or after-shave lotion on a man, you are not supposed to be smelly at all. . . . On the whole, most of us prefer each other to be odoriferously anonymous. . . . As G.K. Chesterton put it—

> They haven't got no noses,
> And goodness only knowses
> The noselessness of man. [20]

Watts and Chesterton here underscore Stevens' poem and Nietzsche's aphorism. The suggestion seems to be that we may have lost the scent, that we may have at some point, unwittingly, been deprived of our nose, so to say, and that without a nose, thinking may be *mere* thought, lacking vigor, like an aesthetic that is airy and aesthete, void of soul and body, not rude enough or grotesque enough to account for an inward journey, one which, in spite of us, has long since had to forfeit the gloss of life and has had to serve in more humble fashion life's essential texture. To round out a realistic sense of things with its putrifying stinks, its burly smells, and its gustiness, a recovery of the sense of smell, a rediscovery of the nose, may be crucial.

If this be the point of those—like Joyce, Stevens, Nietzsche, Heidegger, Watts, and Chesterton—who write on the image of the nose, it is certainly also the point of those who link the image of the clown to thinking about Christ. It may well be no accident, however unintentional, that Harvey Cox wrote, "our *noses* were itching," when he was arguing for a bit more realistic earthiness in religious thinking. The coincidence is striking enough to motivate more musing about it.

Yet, to take the nose as a serious topic may seem as little promising, as comically unserious, as connecting Christ and clowns. To be sure, there is little mystery about the ordinary nose which, as one says, is "plain as the nose on one's face." But this is just the problem. What is plain and ordinary seems lacking in mystery, in gusto and vigor, in the sort of thing clowns are well at home in, whether they like it or not. Clowns and noses may stand in need of re-imagining, re-sensing, re-facing. One might, for example, think a bit about a particular nose, one already uncanny, deeply strange, and one to which the poet writing about Crispin has given clue: namely, *the round, red one on the clown's white face.*

This nose may at first seem a far cry from our own. But, on the other hand, it may turn out to be as disconcertingly near to us as our very own jugular vein. Were this the case, and if the clue of Harvey Cox is not misleading, this nose might even prompt a recovery of a suprising intimacy between Christ and self!

10 THE IMAGE OF THE CLOWN AND SMELL'S DRUNK SENSE

TAKE the case of Hans Schnier. He is the central character of Heinrich Böll's novel, *The Clown*. This "collector of moments," as he calls himself, has an unusual ability. "Not only do I suffer from depression and headaches," he confesses, "but I also have another, almost mystical peculiarity: I can detect smells through the telephone."[1] For example, after speaking about one of his performances with the head of a Christian Education Society, Schnier has to clean his teeth and gargle with cognac. The man had given off "a sickly odor of violet cachous."[2] On the occasion of another telephone call, Schnier says his mother's maid "smelled very nice . . . just of soap, and a little fresh nail polish,"[3] whereas at the end of a conversation with his mother, the clown reported:

> She smelled as she always smelled: of nothing. One of her convictions is: "A lady gives off no odor of any kind either, but she looks as though she would smell nice.[4]

Böll's clown has a remarkable nose!

One other instance of this nasal sense in the novel comes when Schnier is speaking with an anonymous figure at a monastery where his brother, Leo, lives. On first calling there Schnier was disappointed.

> I had been expecting a gentle nun's voice, smelling of weak coffee and dry cake, instead: a croaking old man, and it smelled of pipe tobacco and cabbage, so penetratingly that I began to cough.[5]

Later, however, the telephone-odor was different. "He was smoking a cigar now, and the smell of cabbage was less pronounced."[6]

The conversation between the monk and the clown is important to the novel, containing, as it does, a Biblical saying that appears at the beginning of the book as an epigraph. The monk speaks first:

> "You are an unbeliever, aren't you? Don't say no: I can tell from your voice that you are an unbeliever. Am I right?"
> "Yes," I said.
> "That makes no difference, no difference at all," he said, "there is a place in Isaiah which St. Paul even quotes in the Epistle to the Romans. Listen carefully: To whom he was not spoken of, they shall see: and they that have not heard shall understand." He gave a wicked little laugh. "Did you get it?"
> "Yes," I said with a sigh.
> He raised his voice: "Good evening, sir, good evening," and hung up.[7]

The saying from the Bible, which occurs in both Isaiah 52:12 and in Romans 15:21, is echoed at other places in Scripture. The prophet Isaiah (chapter 6, verse 9) is directed by the Lord to "go and say to this people: 'Hear and hear, but do not understand; see and see, but do not perceive.'" Mark utilizes this prophecy (chapter 4, verse 10) in order to describe the function of Jesus' parables in teaching religious meaning. This Gospel says that Jesus taught "that they may indeed see but not perceive, and may indeed hear but not understand." From these texts one may assume that deep and ultimate significance in life comes in some way other than through the "eyes" and "ears." Perhaps, in a manner of speaking, it is "smelled." This would account for the monk's saying to the clown, Schnier, that he had already sensed it, since after all he had quite an ability for "smell."

There is more, however, to Böll's fantasy than a long-distance nose and a cryptic Biblical comment. The cognac-gargle is a clue. Schnier admits at the beginning of the book that "for the past three weeks I had been drunk most of the time . . . and yesterday, in Bochum, before an audience of young people, I slipped in the middle of a Chaplin imitation and couldn't get up." [8] He never recovers during the entire course of the novel.

Schnier drank because the "remedies for pain" that he had formerly used—the Tantum Ergo or the Litany of Loreto (that is, religion)—no longer worked. So now he says: "There is one temporarily effective remedy: alcohol." He also says: "There could be a permanent cure: Marie." His love has left him. Both religion and love have abandoned the clown in this book. And, as he himself puts it, "a clown who takes to drink falls faster than a drunk tile-layer topples off a roof." [9]

The novel ends feelingly at Carnival time with the fallen clown in front of the Hamburg train station, face made up in white, and one imagines a nose red from drink, singing, *ora pro nobis*, "pray for us."

But this is not quite the end of the story. We have already noted that Schnier calls his nasal ability "mystical," that curiously his unbelief has a religious quality to it, and that his final clown act is a prayer said in the secular marketplace during a pagan festival. Two of Schnier's own sayings make the additional point on their own. He says:

> Sometimes I get a feeling of wonderful emptiness like when I play parchesi when it has gone on for more than three or four hours; just the sounds, the rattle of the dice, the taptap of the little men, the click when one is taken.[10]

And again:

> Think of nothing. Not of cabinet and catholon. Think of the
> clown who weeps in the bath, and whose coffee drips onto his
> slippers.[11]

The aesthetic of Böll's clown, like that of Stevens' Crispin in
the last chapter, is "rude," to be sure. But it is "round," too. It
"rounds" things out, as Stevens' poem said. The "rounding-out"
is the making of a total earthy complex that gathers together a
certain dark intoxication, a grotesque religiosity, a mystical
fallenness. And these are constellated around the image of the
clown's nose, as if they somehow belonged together. This complex is not uncommon in literature. For example, there is a
similar insight concerning the connection between smell and
drunkenness and religion in the poetry of William Blake, where
he writes:

Into the wine presses of Luvah; howling for the clusters
Of human families thro' the deep; the wine presses were fill'd;
The blood of life flow'd plentiful. Odors of life arose
All round the heavenly arches, and the Odors rose singing this song:

"O terrible wine presses of Luvah! O caverns of the grave!
How lovely the delights of those risen again from death!
O trembling joy! excess of joy is like excess of grief."
So sang the Human Odors round the wine presses of Luvah.[12]

Like Blake's lines, the total imaginal complex of Böll's novel
implies that the clown's nose senses through drink, through
failed belief, through the experience of ego's nothing, something that otherwise might not be sensed, a something that lacking in "smell" we might deny or miss. It is like Stevens' saying,
"It made him see how much / Of what he saw he never saw at
all."

But what is that "something" we are missing?

11 A RED NOSE ON WHITE: THE CLOWN'S ARCHETYPAL FACE

THE testimony of the German novelist, Heinrich Böll, is by no means unique. His book about a clown is an imaginal summation of a long tradition. There is recurring witness to the experience of the nose on the white face becoming red and round through drink. This nose achieves the ability to smell in the midst of life's nothing. Indeed, the ability may result from the emptiness itself. It is an archetypal image—this spot of red that appears where color has left, where personal ego has faded. The image appears traditionally in the history of the make-up of the circus clown. It is a tradition worth noting: noses to remember!

Most recently the image has been darkened. The clown's white face and red nose have been shadowed with some black, as for example in the case of the tramp clowns of our century: Otto Griebling from Holland; Emmett Kelly, Sr., from Missouri; Linon, the Swiss who doubled for Jimmy Durante in the film

Dumbo, by Walt Disney. There were also Paul Jerome and Joe Jackson.[1] And one could hardly neglect to mention W. C. Fields, who first attracted the attention of the Marx Brothers with his tramp-clown act.

The tramp make-up was introduced in America by Charles Burke as early as 1882. It seemed from the beginning to be the darkening of a familiar clown-face, namely, that of the *Auguste* (Italian, *toni;* Russian, *r'izhii*). The *Auguste* was originated by Tom Belling in Berlin about 1869. It featured a white face with a red, rubber-ball nose. Americans saw this make-up on Paul Jung, Lou Jacobs, Silvers Oakley, Felix Adler, Gijon Polidor, and—at the Hippodrome in New York City—Marceline. In Europe the make-up was standard with the German clown Grock (a colloquial pronunciation of "grog"), with the Italian Rhum (whose real name was Enrico Sprocani), and with the Frenchman Albert Fratellini (who played the *Auguste* opposite his brothers, taking the pratfalls from their clever, roguish pranks).

The red-nosed, white-faced clown often paired his act with a witty type (compare pages 47f above). Francesco Caroli modified the make-up slightly by using only the red nose while his brother, Ernesto, wore white-face paint and a white conical hat. Footit, whose real name was Theodor Hall, had both white face and red nose, but he played in England opposite a black man named Chocolat. Joseph Grimaldi acted the *Auguste,* but painted the red spots on the face at places other than the nose. Such were the variations in the type.

Nor is it accurate to imply that the *Auguste* marks the beginning of the red nose on the white face. It is an old tradition. Already in the Roman *commedia dell'arte* the nose was important to the clown, as one sees in masks of the character Pantaloon, whose nose is hooked and enlarged. The figure of Bucco the Braggart in the Atelian farce had a soft, round nose, and he often played opposite Dossennus, whose nose was long and hooked.

Neither is the clown's archetypal nose limited to Occidental imagination. To this day bumpkin clowns of Szechuan in China (*yen-tzu-ch'ou*) redden the nose on a white streaked face. The False Face Society of Iroquois clowns uses masks which show grotesquely altered and colored noses. The Pueblo *koyemsi* and the Hopi *kachinas* paint the nose with reddish-brown berry-paint. It would seem that the image has a universal sense, as if this make-up, unlike that of the cosmetologist, were not covering the true face, but rather were revealing some deep face beneath our personal ones, something there to be "faced," to be "made up" in our "make-up."

The Native American examples bring forcibly to mind the connection of this image with drunkenness, as in Böll's literary example. The Hopi *kachinas* clownishly intrude on sacred ceremonies, pretending their interruption to be a result of their drunkenness. Further, the very names of the famous European *Augustes*—Rhum, Porto, and Cognac—make the same association. Ducrow, the nineteenth-century English clown, performed a drunken version of Punch and Judy, an act that explicitly transformed Punch into a drunken Silenos. Matthew Popperton's famous roust-about, "A Trip to Switzerland," featured a moment in which there was an attempt to light a candle while drunk. Charles Burke's tramp was driven to drink in his act, and the German term *Auguste* itself has connotations of drunkenness. And again, need one do more than mention the name W. C. Fields?!

Even outside the circus ring, alcohol seems precariously close to the clown. Many tragic anecdotes could be cited, but two will suffice to make the point. The great American clown, Dan Rice, was ruined by drink. He then became a teetotaler and lectured on the temperance circuit, performing at the end of his life only occasionally in circuses. Charlie Chaplin is another instance. The model for his famous Little Tramp, as biographies often mention, was his alcoholic father.[2]

The red nose on the whitened face seems to belong to drink.

Drunkenness is a clown-act. It produces a remarkable nose, and, curiously, its image relates to religion, as Böll's novel hints. A classical Hindu text on drama, *The Natyasastra,* tells of a buffoon, Vidusaka, who plays opposite the clever rogue, Vita. The former says: "Blessed are those that are drunk with drink; blessed are those that are soaked with drink; blessed are those that are washed with drink; blessed are those that are choked with drink!" [3]

These words from South Asia might have as well been spoken by Shakespeare's Falstaff, who not only sported a red nose himself but who also said of his low-bred associate, Bardolph, that he was "Knight of the Burning Lamp." He said this because the swaggerer's nose had a quality not unlike that of Santa's Rudolph! This point about Bardolph was used by Nathaniel Hawthorne in his work *Fanshawe.* The American writer was describing Hugh Crombie, landlord of the Hand and Bottle Tavern. He wrote: "The tip of his nose glowed with a Bardolphian fire—a flame indeed which Hugh was so far a vestal as to supply with its necessary fuel at all seasons of the year." [4]

What is perhaps most striking in all this is that it relates to a very old mythic source. Crombie, Bardolph, and Falstaff; Vidusaka and the *kachinas; Auguste* and tramp; even Hans Schnier—all these have a prototype for their archetypal faces. Virgil's *Sixth Eclogue* tells of a figure who is "asleep in a cave, veins swollen, as always, with yesterday's wine." Satyrs throw garlands of flowers around him, entrapping him in hopes of a song or a teaching, for he was the teacher of gods. We have met him before in this book. It is Silenos, of course. But now we can note that Virgil reports something unusual about his behavior. Before he began to teach, the Naiads painted his face (can we doubt it is the nose?) with elderberry paint of crimson color (*sanguineis,* the Latin text says)! [5]

Those clowns know something! They carry the silenic tradition of wisdom on their faces. It is a wisdom that might be put this way: if there be no drunkenness, there shall be no sense of smell, no gusto or vigor in thinking, no aroma in life, no knowledge of the gods, no fire in the face, no red with the white, no comedy in our rings. There is a drunk tramp deep in the circus of our selves, something there to be faced. It is, as Crispin found out on his inward journey, a rude aesthetic. But what does it mean? What is it that is being imagined in all this? What is being sensed by this curious, clownish nose that persists so?

12 NASAL FANTASIA 1: PSYCHOLOGY

PSYCHOLOGISTS seem to have ideas about the nose and its varieties of meaning. It is to them, first, that we turn for help with this clownish image.

Wilhelm Fliess was a friend of Freud in 1892 and 1893. Fliess, during this period, wrote two articles in which he identified what he took to be a "reflex neurosis" that had its origin in the nose. He was writing as a medical doctor with a specialty in the nose and throat, and his fantasy, or, as he would have said, his theory, was that headaches, neuralgic pains in the arms, shoulders, ribs, heart, stomach, spleen, lower back, and kidneys, as well as disturbed functions of the digestive organs, heart, and respiratory system, all were traceable to the nose. Fliess said:

> The number of symptoms adduced is great, and yet they owe their existence to one and the same locality—the nose. For their homogeneity is demonstrated, not only by their simultaneous appearance, but by their simultaneous disappearance.[1]

It is indeed a fact that Fliess found he could make the great number of psychological and physical symptoms disappear by treating the nose. It was a simple matter and perhaps not too surprising in retrospect. Fliess administered cocaine to the nasal membrane and, *mirabile dictu,* all was "cured"!

As years went on Fliess linked everything to the nose. He began to view the nose as the whole body, and he was especially fascinated with the connections he observed between the nose and the male and female genitalia, how there could be vicarious nose-bleeding in place of menstruation, how the turbinate bone swelled during miscarriage, and how delivery pains and nasal dysmenorrhea connect, to name only a few of the correspondences. Literally speaking, Fliess' theories were entirely discredited. He was thought to be mad. But as fantasy, his notions seem not totally removed from what is imaginally expressed in the traditional perspectives of clowning and its make-up.

Freud became interested in Fliess' theories. On May 25, 1895, Freud wrote telling Fliess that Breuer had (in Freud's words!) "accepted the whole of your nose." He had written earlier, in another curious sentence, that he "hoped the nasal reflex neurosis will soon be generally known as Fliess' disease" (!).²

Ultimately Freud rejected "the grandoise conception of Wilhelm Fliess," as he called it in the work *Beyond the Pleasure Principle.* Apparently he saw the madness of it, that it was too literalistic about causal connections between mind and body. The two men broke off their close personal relationship for many reasons, to be sure, but part of the break happened in 1901 when Fliess insisted on the physical accuracy of what Freud took to be psychological. Freud saw that it is not just a matter of the nose on the face, but rather a case of the psychological nose that is yet to be "faced."

And yet . . . yet Fliess' fantasy keeps the matter physical and crude, which is the perspective, also, of the clown's behavior.

Such physicality keeps body in the psychology, keeps the nose in the thinking and the feeling. We might even say: it keeps it all drunk on coke.

Otto Fenichel, on the other hand, sided with Freud, and in sober fashion, indeed. His article, "The Long Nose," though it be psychological in the extreme, is as literalistic as Fliess, even if less crazy. It discloses a second fantasy about the nose.[3]

Fenichel's particular interest is the scornful gesture of making what is called "a long nose," that is, thumbing one's nose at another person. Like sticking out the tongue, it lengthens in a gesture a part of the body which already is characterized by the fact that it protrudes. Following Freud, Fenichel immediately associates this gesture with the penis. His problem is to account for why the gesture functions to show scorn. That is, why, if one wants to heap abuse on someone else, or to suggest that another person is in some way impotent, why would he exhibit precisely a potent phallus, symbolically speaking, a nose that is lengthened, stiff, and waving?

Fenichel's reasoning is clever, if also fantastic. He first notes that the exhibitionist gesture occurs in fact more often in cases of girls than of boys. He then shows that studies reveal these girls to suffer from father-complexes and from a sense of castration. It then becomes a simple matter to deduce that the gesture is a projection or compensation. It says: "Look what a long penis *you* have, and yet you are still powerless to get me!" Ultimately, this show of strength is a sign of weakness. It indicates having to compensate for a lack with the hand substituting for what one would like to have.

This is not the place to decide for or against the merit of Fenichel's idea as a psychological "theory," but as fantasy it is fascinating in relation to the clown's nose which has, in its traditional make-up, been reddened, rounded, and softened. From Fenichel's perspective the clown's appearance seems to suggest that what is long, like the nose, is actually round and soft. What is aggressive is in fact weak. What attempts heroically to dominate is important to smell. We have noses, but they are an embarrassment. They are the point at which we are clowns.[4]

Marie-Louise von Franz has still a third notion about the nose. Her idea is thoroughly psychological, but its psychology, unlike Fenichel's, comes from the imaginal world of soul. It is rooted in a fairy tale.

Von Franz is discussing the folk-tale called "The Loyal and Disloyal Ferdinand."[5] In that story a king who has no nose falls prey to destructive ideas. This is a theme well-known in fairy tales. One can read in this literature of noses cut off as punishments for breaking a law and as instances of the fulfillment of a wish. Some persons come to birth through the nose, while others are resuscitated through the nose. Ogres are characterized by their monstrous noses. In one story the Devil dies of a nose-bleed resulting from overheat. There is an Icelandic tale about a person whose nose has become crooked, and there is a Jewish story about those who have no noses at all.[6]

In the particular case of the King and Disloyal Ferdinand, von Franz observes that the nose represents the function of intuition. The nose is the organ that "smells out" something, as for example one says that a stock broker uses his "nose" or that someone "smells a rat." The nose functions to keep us in touch with psyche, with soul.

During the course of human evolution certain animal abilities have been sacrificed to the end of higher development of species. So our sense of smell is inferior to that of many animals. For example, our mucous membrane covers only five square centimeters whereas that of a German Shepherd dog covers one hundred and fifty square centimeters. The dog has two hundred and twenty million cells with which to smell, whereas we have only five million.[7] But, as von Franz notes, the loss of a capacity at a literal level may enable it to return in a psychological way. This is to say, the psychological "nose" may help us to get some intuition and instinct, some soul and body, into our thinking and feeling. Perhaps this, too, is part of what the clown's make-up indicates.

But care must be taken at just this point lest we somehow lose the nose in the theories. The fantasies of our nasality—that it is our whole body, that it is our sexuality, that it is psychological intuition—can become ways of avoiding the rude, grotesque aesthetic of the clown. Theories can function as defense mechanisms, even when they are accurate. Amplifications can, as it were, deodorize the rancid stench of life. Thinking thereby would lose its aroma, its smell. What we need, perhaps, is not so much images of the nose provided by psychologists, but rather a nasal way of imagining.

This is the achievement of the fairy tale, and it is also the work of other literature: to help us get the nose back into it, keeping our noses to the grindstone, forcing us to stick with the image rather than running it too quickly into theory or idea, into the thinking of our eyes and ears, or into the feelings of our taste and touch. Poets, novelists, and dramatists give us the sense. Their art puts us onto the scent, as we shall see next.

13 NASAL FANTASIA 2: LITERATURE

WHEN thinking about the nose Pinocchio comes to mind. But Collodi's character carries a motif different from the one related to the clown's nose. Pinocchio's nose gets lengthened, not reddened, from lying, and though lengthening and lying may be indirectly relevant, this particular aesthetic is hardly rude enough for the tradition of the clown.

Nor is Cyrano's nose to the point. Both the seventeenth century historical swaggerer and Edmond Rostand's nineteenth-century dramatic counterpart, Cyrano de Bergerac, occasion defensiveness and heroic duelling, a whitening of the face of others in the face of the reddening of one's own. Here red and white are split rather than wed, as in the clown's face. For this latter the works of James Joyce, Laurence Sterne, and Nikolai Vasilievich Gogol seem more to the point.

In *Finnegans Wake*, James Joyce relates the word "nose" to a clownish sense and to drunkenness. For example:

I can telesmell him H_2CE_3 that would take a township's breath away! Gob and I nose him too well as I do meself. . . . And the laughing jackass. Harik! Harik! Harik! The rose is white in the darik! And Sunfella's nose has got rhinoceritis from haunting the roses in the parik! So all rogues lean to rhyme. And contradrinking themselves. . . .[1]

Here we have the red and white, the alcohol, and the long-distance smell. But Joyce's passage indicates also the sense of it. It has to do with a pun between the body-part, the nose, and the verb, "to know." What makes the pun possible is a "lean rhyme," or "learning to rhyme." This suggests that imaginal language links the archetypal image of the drunk clown and his nose to a particular way of knowing, a way of sensing poetically by way of image, joke, and pun.

Indeed, the nose/knows pun continues regularly throughout the book. For example, we read: "Matrosenhosens nose the joke."[2] "His own fitther couldn't nose him."[3] Joyce has a word for this nasal, poetic knowing. He calls it the "sounddance," and he connects it to psychological and mythological knowing in a well-known passage from the novel:

In the buginning is the woid, in the muddle is the sounddance and thereinofter you're in the unbewised again, vund vulsyvolsy. You talker dunsker's brogue men we our souls speech obstruct hostery . . . . Talk of Paddybarke's echo! Kick nuck, Knockcastle! Muck! And you'll nose it, O you'll nose it, without warnward from we.[4]

According to this passage, the nose's way of knowing, of catching the scent, is something that will hit us when we are in the "muddle" of life, after some "void" happens to us. It will be a "word" that will "bug" us and begin to lead us to the language of "soul" which we too often "obstruct."

Joyce speaks further of this "woid" that we experience in our various "voids" by saying:

Herenow chuck english and learn to pray plain. Lean on your lunch. No cods before Me. Practice preaching. Think in your stomach. . . . Let earwigger's wivable teach you the dance.[5]

The tone, as well as the content, are reminiscent of the traditional clown.

If Joyce expresses a *knowing* by the body, Sterne's work, *Tristram Shandy,* imagines a nose as the *body* of our knowings. Sterne's imaginal sense is a second version of the archetypal image.

The novelist begins, perhaps ironically, by insisting that "by the word *Nose*, throughout all this long chapter of noses, and in every other part of my work where the word *Nose* occurs,—I declare, by that word I mean a Nose, and nothing more, or less." [6] We say "perhaps ironically" because only a few pages later Tristram's father tells brother Toby: "I'll study the mystic and the allegoric sense [of long noses]," [7] as if, in spite of the protestation to the contrary, the word "nose" may have other meanings.

This possibility becomes more realized in the novel when we read that "a long nose is not without domestic conveniences also, for that in a case of distress,—and for want of a pair of bellows, it will do excellently well, *ad excitandum focum* (to stir up the fire)." [8] Not only can one stir up a fire with a long nose (!), but Tristram feels disgraced by the shortness of his nose,[9] inasmuch as it was mashed by the forceps of Dr. Slop (!) at his birth,[10] an event that Tristram himself links to his name (meaning "melancholy"),[11] as well as to his accidental circumcision which came as a result of a window sash accidently falling on him! [12]

The implicit connection (or is it already more than obvious?) between the nose and the genital organ is made clearly explicit in the novel when Slawkenbergius's tale of how the people of Strasbourg lost control of their city is related. The people had all left town, crossing the bridge on the road to Frankfurt, to get a voyeuristic glimpse of the unbelievably large "nose" of a passing stranger. Certainly it is possible that a "nose" should have been that large. Slawkenbergius says that "there is no cause in nature why a nose might not grow to the size of a man himself." [13] But an innkeeper thinks it all some sort of imposture. He says skeptically that the "thing" was in fact probably dead. The innkeeper's wife, on the other hand, had another fantasy! "'Tis a live nose," she said, "and if I am alive myself, . . . I will touch it!" [14] So goes the tale of Slawkenbergius, concluding with the exclamation: "It is not the first—and I fear not the last fortress that has been either won—or lost by Noses!" [15]

If there be any remaining doubt as to the sense of the "nose" in *Tristram Shandy*, Ambrose Paraeus' theory concerning the length of noses surely puts that doubt to rest. It all has to do, he says, with the quality of the nurse's breast.

> As the flatness and shortness of *puisne* noses was due to the firmness and elastic repulsion of the same organ of nutrition in the hale and lively,—which, though happy for the woman, was the undoing of the child, inasmuch as his nose was so snubbed, so rebuffed, so rebated, and so refrigerated thereby, as never to arrive *ad mensuram suam legitimam;*—but that in case of the flaccidity and softness of the nurse or mother's breast,—by sinking into it, quoth Paraeus, as into so much butter, the nose was comforted, nourished, plumped up, refreshed, refocillated, and set a-growing forever.[16]

So, in the fantasies of the Shandy family, the nose's sense is surrogate for our bodily, generative sexuality, though it is this not without considerable humor and some grotesqueness.

It is this last, the gothic and grotesque, which prompted Gogol's odd short-story called simply, "The Nose." "On March 25," we are told, "an unusually strange incident happened in St. Petersburg." [17] The reader hardly needs be told that it is strange. A barber, who is also a blood-letter, awakes to find baked in his breakfast bread a nose that he at once recognizes as belonging to that of one of his customers, a Major Kovalyov! Simultaneously, Kovalyov awakes to find his nose missing!

During the plot of the story the barber tries to get rid of the nose that has intruded in his food. He wraps it in a rag and drops it from a bridge. But a policeman spots him. Meanwhile,

Kovalyov goes in quest of his missing nose. As for the nose itself—according to the tale—it takes on a life of its own, having the habit of parading every afternoon at 3:00 o'clock on Nevsky Street while crowds gather to watch.

At last the policeman returns the nose to its proper owner. But the nose fails to adhere to Kovalyov's face. Only when a proper length of time has passed—two weeks to the minute—does the nose, on its own, return to lie between the Major's cheeks. It is clearly recognizable to him by the pimple that was at the left nostril on the day before its departure!

The author remarks at the end of this strange story that "no matter what anyone says, such things do happen in this world—not often, but they do happen."

What happens in this world, but not often, according to Gogol's fantasy, is that the "nose" leaves us sometimes and it sometimes returns. Or, from the barber's point of view, "noses" sometimes come to our breakfasts, uninvited, and we try to rid ourselves of them. Or, to put it still another way, what goes and comes, as if on its own—drawing here also on Joyce and Sterne—is the sense of body, of sexuality, of knowledge that carries with it erotic or intuitive dimensions. Such may show itself in the morning, or it may be missing when we look in a mirror. If we wanted to find it, we had better look at that which is most grotesque in our feelings and in our fantasies . . . or so suggests this odd literature about the "nose."

It is not that Gogol, Sterne, and Joyce show us something that Von Franz, Fenichel, and Fliess do not. On the contrary, it must be already obvious that Gogol's grotesquery matches that of Fliess, Sterne's sexuality is expressed by Fenichel, and Joyce's way of "nosing" is precisely what Von Franz calls psychological intuition. Far from denying the theoretical fantasies about the "nose," the literary examples corroborate that there is a proper "nose" in them.

The difference, of course, lies in the *manner* of expression. The literary use of pun, metaphor, and grotesquery helps us to get a real sense for the truly dramatic life that lurks in thinking. The fictions of the artists make the thinking of the psychologists drunk and crazy. By showing the drunkenness and craziness they give an aroma, a smell to what is thought and felt, just as Nietzsche hoped. They demonstrate that it is not so much that our noses are Freudian penises or Jungian intuition as that our sexuality, our body, and our psychic sense are all somehow nasal. That is, the literature does not commend that we discover sex or soul with our nose as it notes that we are already "nosing" about with our bodies and our psyches, that there is a kind of knowing and feeling going on in our sexuality and in our imagination of which we may be unaware, lacking, as we often do, a nose for it.

But the clown's nose knows what the literature helps us to experience: namely, that where there is drunkenness in the thought and feeling, there may be a round, red nose with a remarkable sense.[18]

The point is not that we all need be clowns or poets. The point—and not always a pretty one!—is rather that we are drunk and crazy already in some *psychological* sense, though it may take clown and poet to help us see the grotesque clown and rude, realistic poetry in us all. It would find considerable intuition in the grotesque places of self. It may even discover some comedy in the tramp who inhabits our psychic circus rings. It may find a little red spot in the white, a ruddy, rude aesthetic in pale ego's lack of sense. It may recover a nose precisely in the pratfalls of life. It may rub our noses in it, and thereby round and redden them.

After all, a nose is a wonderful thing! Containing little coils of arteries, ducts and blood vessels, as it does, it raises to body temperature the air that gives us life, moistening on the cilia hairs of the soft, mucous membrane a *spiritus* from which we would otherwise die a death of airy pneumonia. As a result of its circuitous passages, the nose enables us to smell inhaled breath, but not noxious exhaled odors of our own personal-ego breathings. It lets the fluids pass by way of paranasal sinuses, with which it also connects to our tear's lacrimal ducts. Its olfactory receptors, unlike the buds of taste which only handle four senses—salt, sweet, sour, and bitter—detect innumerable odors, thereby differentiating the infinity which not only taste, but also sight, touch, and hearing confuse. In short, the nose warms and moistens that which gives us life, bringing it in and down, individuating spirit into soul by way of body.

Warming the cold, and moistening the dry!—perhaps this is what the clown knows, what his nose wants of us.

14 THE SMELL OF TRADITIONAL RELIGION AND ITS MYTHIC UNDER-ODOR

IT MAY well seem that we have come a long distance from Christ, meandering, as we have, through meditations on facial make-up and fantasia about noses. We began by observing that some writers in our time are exploring "a new iconography of Christ," connecting Him with the figure of the clown. But have our subsequent chapters demonstrated in any way how and why this connection is worth making even if it were warranted?

The excursions of the last chapters may not have been in vain *if* they could provide clues toward achieving some aroma in religious sensibility, a fragrance, as it were, in theological thinking, some warmth for and a moistening of spiritual ideas. This very sentiment was expressed in a London magazine, *The Temple Bar*, dating from 1862. It said: "A noseless face would have no divinity." [1] There is also that curious remark by St. Paul: "We are the aroma of Christ to God among those who are being saved and among those who are perishing, to one a fragrance from death to death, to the other a fragrance from life to life." [2]

St. Paul was likely alluding to incense, using this allusion metaphorically in relation to life. Perhaps if we were to inquire into religion's use of the smell of incense, the connection of all that has gone before to an "aroma of Christ" would become more explicit. It is hoped that an inquiry will even lead our thinking about Christ nearer to the sensibility of the clown and his face. We aim, strange as it may sound to say so, not only at an image of Christ the Clown, but, in St. Paul's sense, at a Nasal Christ, Christ the Nose, by whom the person may not only see and hear, touch and feel, but also "smell" his way through life christianly.

In the Hebrew Bible there are forty-seven references to odors and they all have to do with incense. Thirty-five of these references occur in the books of Numbers and Leviticus. They are prescriptions for worship.[3] Proper worship of God, it is implied, consists in making pleasant smells for God or for the gods. According to one hadith, the prophet Mohammed said of himself, "Three things have been dear to me: women, prayer, pleasant odors!" [4]

This is a more radical matter than it might at first seem. St. Paul's suggestion is that we ourselves are the incense, and that our "odor" has to do with life and death ("a fragrance from death to death, . . . from life to life"). It is as if life and death have a smell. Indeed, many Biblical texts speak of having life or obtaining life through the nose. There are passages in Genesis to this effect (Genesis 2:7; 7:22), and Job attests that "the spirit of God is in my nostrils" (Job 27:3), by which he seems to mean that he has life in the midst of his many sufferings. Philo, commenting on Abraham's father Terah, notes that this latter's name means "scent exploring," that is, following his nose. So Terah died in Haran, which Philo calls a "sort of mother-city of senses." Philo makes his point with an image:

Just as we are told that hounds used in the chase have by nature the sense of smell especially keen, so that by following the scent they can track out and find the dead bodies of wild animals at the greatest distance, in the same way does the man who is enamoured of discipline follow the path of the sweet effluvium given forth by justice and other virtues.

Such persons, according to Philo, are ones who use their "noses." They "will be quickened and enkindled," he says, "with breaths of virtue." [5] The "nose," it seems, gives spiritual life.

But according to the Bible the nose means death, too. In Second Samuel an angry God breathes fire from his mouth and smoke from his nostrils (II Samuel 22:9, 16). This is like the rebuke of God in Psalm 18, verses 8 and 15. It comes through God's nose (compare Job 41:20 and Isaiah 65:5)! Also, in the Song of Moses, God floods the Pharoah's men with "a blast of ... . nostrils" (Exodus 15:8). The story of Jesus raising Lazarus from the dead indicates that death can be smelled (John 11:39), and it may be recalled that the Magi brought a gift of frankincense to the child Jesus. This is a spice which, with myrrh, is used as an incense in embalming the dead.

In the image of the nose, then, life and death come together as two aspects of one gift. The word "incense" itself carries this basic ambivalence. The Old French terms, *incenser* and *encenser,* and the Latin word *incensus,* are formed with a past participle of *incendere,* which means, "to set on fire." Thus, if one were to say that God is "incensed," it could mean that He is angry and/or that He is made to smell good. When the nose is "incensed" it glows and burns (Latin, *candere*), and there is both life and death in that redness.

Incense, then, is not a cosmetic to cover death, but, from this Biblical Perspective, it alerts us to the odor of death, the smell being already a lively sense, a sense for life. In the Havdalah, the ritual of parting from the Sabbath, the worshipper is told to praise God with the over-flowing spice-box. The meaning is that the aroma will continue throughout the week, carrying the smell of religion into the everyday world, as if the *smells* of everydayness were somehow clues to religious meaning in life. If this were indeed so, it would be a disaster were Psalm 115 accurate in saying: "They have . . . noses, but do not smell." [6] One might say that without a nose a person could never be properly incensed.

In addition to incense there is another "smell" in the history of religion. Between the tenth and nineteenth centuries an uncanny "fact" was reported from time to time. One reads of it, for example, in: *Selectum martyra acta,* IV.iii.198f; Baeda's *Ecclesiastical History,* III.viii; Malory's *Morte d'Arthur,* XXI.xii; Fioretti's *Opera,* XLVIII.66b; Bossuet's *Universal History,* I.270; and Voltaire's obscene poem about Joan of Arc, *La Pucelle,* I.22. What is reported is that an *odeur de sainteté,* "an odor of sanctity," is noticed coming from the bodies of dead saints. As Swedenborg put it in his work, *Heaven and Hell:* "There was also a sensation of aromatic odor, as of a dead body embalmed, for when the celestial angels are present, what is cadaverous then excites a sensation as of what is aromatic." [7] Dostoievski writes the same about Father Zosima's death in *The Brothers Karamazov,* as does Sir Walter Scott about Ivanhoe. In a classic nineteenth-century work on mysticism, R. A. Vaughan made a small addition to this tradition when he said: "There is an odor of iniquity, you must know, as well as an odor of sanctity." [8]

Whether or not there is "fact" to what is reported is not the point at issue here. The point, rather, is that there is such a tradition, and the tradition itself expresses an important psychological fantasy quite apart from its metaphysical and moral meaning. The fantasy is that religious significance is sensed by smell. This is the same notion which is symbolized in the traditional use of incense in worship. It is basic to religious tradition.

But this idea has an underside to it, a sort of mythological shadow haunting it. This shadow-side may bring us nearer to its meaning for life. Three pagan prototypes of the Biblical and traditional religious images of smelling will be probed to this end.

In Greek myth it is the prophetess Cassandra who knows the deep dimensions of smell. Aeschylus calls her a "keen scented hound," and she herself says, "I scent the trail of bloody guilt." We may say that Cassandra has blood in her nose. It is bloody red. She gasps at one point in the drama, and the chorus says: "You gasp, as if some nausea choked your very soul." This is to say, her nose is, as it were, her way to "soul." But the way is violent, for she says: "There is a smell of murder. The walls drip with blood." The chorus, then, misses her point. It cannot "smell" like she can. So the chorus says: " 'Tis but the odor of the altar sacrifice." They are wrong, of course. Cassandra's prophetic, psychic, soul-nose senses something deeper than incense. There is violence and blood in it. It reeks.[9]

There is something similar to this in the mythology of the Kraho Tribe from South America. According to one of their stories, everyone died at one point in the tribe's primal history because the smell was so bad coming from the "water souls" who are called Kokridho. The people had attempted to put these underworld water-powers in their own personal control, enslaving these souls. But it did not work. On the following night the Kokridho came to the village and everyone died of the smell of the souls.[10]

A Shipaya myth tells of another situation in which the people suffered, not from the smell of the gods, but because they could *not* smell the gods. In primordial times these Indians greeted the wrong one of three canoes which approached. They made the error because they mistook the smell, having been told by the Demiurge to use their noses in differentiating the good from the evil powers.[11]

Claude Lévi-Strauss has shown how common this theme is among North and South American Indian tribes. Opossum and skunk smells among the Catawba in the Carolinas, the

Cherokees and Creek in the Southeast, the Pawnee in the Southwest, not to mention many Amazon peoples, indicated, among other things, a burning and rotting death brought by swarms of flies (fates?), the inundating flood of waters, the tribe's loss of fire, and the abandonment of the people by the gods and souls.[12] These Indians, along with Cassandra, indicate that, in some sense, *the nose is the way that man is able to discover a violence of death which, paradoxically, connects him to a soul-filled life.*

The mythology just cited already implies a second mythic shadow in the fantasies of religion concerning smell. This second dimension is expressed in Greek myth by Hippolytus when he is dying. He says that he smells the goddess Artemis nearby.[13] In his suffering, *Hippolytus knows the goddess by his nose.* The odor is in the pain. His pain is his way of intuiting the complexes of soul which he suffers. These complexes are archetypal. They are expressed in the stories of the gods. The gods have special smells. They can be differentiated by the nose. So it is that there are particular incenses that are to be used for specific deities, according to the Orphic Hymns. There is myrrh for Nereus, storax for Proteus, frankincense for Hermes, and so on.[14]

In Chapter X we saw, in the imagery of a modern novel, that *alcohol was linked to religion and smell.* This is the third mythological motif which shadows traditional religion. The source of this motif is an allusion by the prophet Ezekiel to a practice that is, from his perspective, an "abomination to the Lord."

Ezekiel tells of a people who, as he says, "put the branch (z^emora) to the nose" (Ezekiel 8:17). This phrase may refer to an Egyptian sun-cult, or to the worship of Tammuz-Adonis.[15] It is not altogether clear. But whatever the allusion may be, what is clear is that there was a common religious ritual in the Ancient Near East during which the worshipper put his hand to his nose while holding something. This was a way of meeting the god.

In one cuneiform tablet, for example, Gilgamesh raises a branch to his face while standing before the sun god.[16]

In Ezekiel's account it is a particular branch, the $z^e mora$. According to other passages of Scripture which use this same term, this is the tree of life identified specifically as a vine-stock. In Numbers 13:23 we read: "And they cut from thence a z^e-mora, and from it one bunch of grapes." Other examples of this link between the "branch" and "wine" occur in Ezekiel 15:2, Isaiah 17:10f, Nahum 2:3, etc.[17]

There is yet a further association. Zmr and its cognate words commonly mean "phallus" in the Talmud, as do parallel terms in Arabic and Syriac.[18] All this points to a single complex of meaning which includes the motifs of "nose," "wine," and "phallus." Each implicates the other. The nose is reddened with wine when the branch is put to the nose. The branch is also a phallus which is lifted erect and becomes like the nose. Both nose and phallus are drunk, that is, they are red with intoxication. The intoxication is erotic, and in the eros of intoxication one smells the god. Certainly it is clear how in this complex of meaning Ezekiel's testimony to such pagan mythic practice is prototypical of the imaginal witness of Heinrich Böll's novel with its similar themes.

Ancient myth, then, gives a deep scent to what is implicit in the use of incense and in the tradition of the odor of sanctity which appear in orthodox religious contexts. The myth seems to suggest that there may be an unwittingly psychological link between St. Paul's saying, "We are the aroma of Christ," and Böll's Schnier, the drunk and obscene clown weeping, not over Jerusalem, but in his bathtub. The nose is the clue to the connection, and in order further to see how this clue helps our understanding we might do well to recall the two functions of the actual nose: moistening what is dry, and warming what is cold. The first of these functions, the moistening, is related, as it turns out, intimately to the work of the clown, that is, to the work of wit and humor. It is to this that we turn in the next chapter.

15 MOISTENING: THE HUMOR OF OUR WITS' END

THE word "humor" originally referred to "moisture." To give humor meant to moisten, and to have a sense of humor would be to be able to sense the different moistures of self. From ancient times through the sixteenth century, the "humors" indicated specifically the *four* fluids of the physical body. But beginning with the sixteenth century (though there may have been indications of this here and there before), the fundamental fantasy concerning humor and its connection to moisture became linked more and more to psychological rather than physical characteristics. One can see this tendency, for example, in the writings of Ben Jonson.[1]

The point of this tendency in ideas was to see that one not only could be moistened by humor but that also one could identify a particular humor by the manner of the moistening. If the humor were that of blood, then the mood or psychic characteristic was sanguinity; if phlegm, then phlegmatic; if bile, then choleric or angry; if black bile, then melancholic and depressive. The moistening of the humors gives specific feelings or particular pathic states.[2] So in 1807 one British writer was to say that a person mingles his "feeling with humour and humour with feeling."[3] And John Dennis wrote that "to every passion there is a humour which answers to it."[4] DeQuincey also spoke in this way, saying that "humour is that which is touched by the cross-lights of pathos."[5] So it is, in this view, that the bodily fluids could become metaphors for states of soul, for feelings and passions. This sixteenth-century fantasy seems to suggest that by noticing different sorts of moistures in ourselves we may be able to sense particular varieties of psyche.

About this same time in the history of ideas there came a shift in a second notion: that of "wit." The so-called "wits" had for centuries been thought to be *five* in number. So five specific things were meant when, for example, one of Shakespeare's characters said that he was scared out of his wits,[6] or blessed his wits,[7] or was whipped by his wits,[8] or was brought to his wits,[9] or lost his wits,[10] or was restored to them.[11] A Northumbrian poem of the fourteenth century, the *Cursor mundi,* puts the definition succinctly: "Hering, sight, smelling and fele, cheuing, or wittes five."[12] That is, the five wits were the five senses. The idea here is that my wit comes to me by way of my sense, and that I sense by way of my wits.

But in 1509, Stephen Hawes, in a work called *The Pastime of Pleasure,* identified the wits differently. He said that they were (1) common sense, (2) imagination, (3) fantasy, (4) memory, and (5) conjecture.[13] Now it may be that this change is merely an amplification of what might be meant by the five senses, as if to locate one's sensation one might imagine it, fantasize it, remember it, guess at it, and use a little common sense. To lose one's wits, then, would be to be without these abilities. Indeed, one *could* lose one's imagination, memory, and so on, though of course, one could hardly lose one's humors, one's characteristic moistures, however unconscious one might be of them.

The relation between humors and wits, therefore, can provide a way of understanding the image of the nose on the clown's face. If it is by one's wits that one senses, imagines, fantasizes, remembers, and guesses at the varieties of moisture in the self, one's differing characteristics, moods, passions and feelings, then one may think of the clown's nose as his wit-way. It would be his manner of finding the drunkenness and intoxication, a way of locating the little red roundness in an otherwise white leukemic life. Through the wits (all five of them!) one knows where and how to express the humors (all four of them!) while yet preserving their moisture, not drying it out, conserving both body and soul, grotesque and erotic.

Yet it was these very wits which were lost in the history of the evolution of ideas. In the seventeenth and early eighteenth centuries humor and wit came to be viewed as distinct from each other. It became a matter of either/or: either wit or humor, rather than wit being the *sense of* humor. Congreve, in 1695, noted how often wit was mistaken for humor, as if they were completely different from each other. Humor, he thought, is the soul of drama, not wit. Like Shakespeare's Benedick, in *Much Ado about Nothing*, Congreve felt that "a college of wit crackers cannot flout me out of my humour." [14] Wit cannot help with humor, or so it came to be thought. Carlyle was another who viewed humor and wit as unrelated, calling wit talent and humor genius, two completely different characteristics in a person.[15] John Dennis, in 1702, came to feel that humor is the true business of comedy, agreeing in this with Congreve. Dennis viewed humor as being linked with human judgment, as opposed to fantasy, which he thought to be characteristic of wit.[16] Dennis made a rhyme which shows his point of view:

> That silly thing men call sheer Wit avoid
> With which our Age so nauseously is cloy'd;
> Humour is all, Wit should be only brought
> To turn agreeably some proper thought.[17]

It was likely inevitable, once the notions of wit and humor were split off from one another, that there would be debate over which were the better. Indeed, not everyone concurred with the opinions of Congreve and Dennis. Shadwell, an English critic who did agree with them, found himself embroiled in controversy with another critic and poet, John Dryden. This latter, in 1671, took the opposite view, favoring wit over humor, in his work, *Preface to an Evening's Love.* Dryden could go so far as to confess that humor instructs us, but he thought it the *proper* work of literature not to instruct but to delight. And that, he asserted, is the work of wit.[18]

Yet in the eighteenth and nineteenth centuries still another thing happened in this history of ideas. Seeing that the notion of wit had been split off from that of humor, some became concerned, during this period of so-called Enlightenment, to get back our wits, as it were. But they did not, as had Dryden in the preceding century, identify wit with delight. Rather, more and more there was a movement afoot to connect wit and reason or thinking. So in an eighteenth-century encyclopedia we read: "Humor is a low and local thing, but wit is high and cosmopolite accomplishment . . . Humor seems to exclude and wit to include the idea of thought." [19]

In two short centuries wit moved from being thought of as *sense* to being imagined as *reason*. Thus, the "wits" could no longer be thought of as plural, being five in number, but were rather thought of as singular, being the same as the single-mindedness of clear thinking. The work of imagination, common sense, fantasy, memory, and conjecture was being replaced by Enlightenment rationalism. Further, wit was not only imagined to be reason, but John Locke and William Hazlitt were to come along and call it "inferior" reason, being subordinated to logic.[20]

It may be noted that humor is lost altogether in this history, and wit becomes *mere* fancy in Locke, imagination in Coleridge, and is replaced finally by intellect in Kant and Hegel. What we are left with is the suffering of an imagined split between thinking and feeling, between reason and passion, the former of these hardly being able to give expression to the latter, as the wits once did for the humors.

Why do we report this? Well, suppose we were to understand this literary and intellectual history, not as moments in Western ideas, but as ways of seeing, ways that could engage our psyche *at any moment* in time. Then far from being an academic tale, the story would have important soul-sense. It might sound something like this:

Sometimes we have our wits about us, and they are experienced as diverse. In common sense, conjecture, imagination, fantasy, and memory we manage to express our several humors of soul, our temperaments, passions, and moods.

But there are other times in life, too. We sometimes choose up sides, as it were, within our very self, electing for common sense, conjecture, imagination, fantasy, or memory, but now cut off from the moisture which flows in us deeply. At such times, our moods are suffered in themselves. They have no way to express themselves. They go on as if having a life of their own. Meanwhile, our wit—now split off from our moisture—is dry, caustic, sharp, and, even when "right," is alienating.[21]

But this is not all. There is yet a third moment in our experience, a sort of schizy time. It comes when we think that common sense, conjecture, fantasy, imagination, and memory all must be reasoned about, thought out, and explained. In this thinking we may notice that our sense and feeling for death's whiteness and for love's drunken redness have no place. We are at the end of our wits, and we have also lost the sense of humor about our humors.

Viewed in this way, what at first may seem a literary history of ideas may also be seen as a story of our souls. In such a perspective this development of fantasies also brings us nearer to the clown's psyche or to a clownish psyche. His face links wit and humor, as least imaginally, when it brings together in the make-up Auguste's humor and Whiteface's wit. The pathos, the feel, of the red nose on the white face is that it shows forth the suffering of some great divorce in soul, a schizophrenia of a split archetypal form. The clown's face makes-up a *coniunctio*, a marriage. It depicts the wit of humors and the humor of wits. His nose moistens.

Perhaps this could be seen as precisely the value of the clown for an incarnational christology, for a carnal theology. The clown shows how to express the moistening: not in reason, whether pure or practical (Kant); not in judgment or will (Schopenhauer); not in absolute Spirit (Hegel); nor in feeling, even in the feeling of Absolute Dependence (Schleiermacher). When we think theologically in these ways about religious meaning, the thinking will not carry the violence, the sex, and the intoxication which we found in mythology as being crucial to religion. Theology loses its wits and the humors go underground, as it were, in unconscious complexes of human fantasy and feeling.

The clown's face suggests we "face" theology in a different way, watching its ideas for common sense, for fantasies about deep human meaning, for imaginal worlds otherwise unthinkable, for deep *memoria*, and for conjectures concerning life. There might be, as Nietzsche hoped, some fragrance in such thinking, perhaps even an "aroma of Christ." As James Joyce put it:

> Mund my achilles, swell my obolum, wosh-up my nase serene ... by turning clement, urban, eugenious and celestian in the mormose of good grogory humours.... That is quite about what I came on *my* missions with *my* intentions laudibiliter to settle with *you*, barbarousse. ... Let Pauline be Irene ... And let me be Los Angeles. Now measure your length. Now estimate my capacity. Well, sour? Is this space of our couple of hours too dimensional for you, temporiser? Will you give up? [22]

16 WARMING: A PHENOMENOLOGY OF STRAIGHT AND ROUND

LIKE our physical noses, the clown's nose moistens our airs, but it also warms them. It not only reveals the blood reddening, the vasal dilation of drink's intoxicating wetness, but it also shows a softening and rounding of what is normally as straight as an erect phallus. In the clown's face, straight becomes round, as if, at least in his perspective, these two belong together.

We have already viewed this straight-round doubleness of the image historically. It was presented in Chapter XI as two characters combined in one facial make-up. The wit of Whiteface was thereby imaginally joined to the humor of Auguste. It is as if the circus clown, in his figure, weds Lear's lean Fool, who is sober yet mad, to Prince Hal's rotund friend, Falstaff, who is the boy's teacher and yet is constantly quite drunk. Or, again, it is like Hermes' phallic herm, erect and straight, constellated with Dionysos' round-dance, meandering and moist. The clown's white face with its long nose now become round is like Silenos who is *at once* fat as Falstaff and yet ithyphallic as some Dionysos. In the person of mythical Silenos, Fool and Falstaff. Hermes and Dionysos, come together. It is the same with the clown's face.

The comic tradition often has presented this constellation of images as a pair. There were crafty Harlequin and melancholy Pierrot who gets slapped; clever Brighella and Scapino, on the one hand, and Pedrolino and Gilles who are rebuffed, on the other; Tambo and Bones; the Chinese Wen and Wu; the Hindu Vidusaka and Vita; the Balinese Penasar and Kartala; the Occidental Mountebank who gets up on a bench and the *zani* ("zany") who are named for foods (Jack Pudding, Jean Potage, Pickel Herring, and Hans Wurst). This tradition of *Döppleganger* and *Widersacher* continues, as we already noted in Part One of this book, like some Cain and Abel, or Jacob and Esau, throughout all time. We mentioned Don Quixote and Sancho Panza, Don Giovanni and Leporello, Laurel and Hardy, Abbott and Costello, Graciosos and Bobo, Burns and Allen, Martin and Lewis, Rowan and Martin, and the Smothers Brothers. Even our language carries the double-sense, speaking, as it does, of a "straight" man and of a "softee." Only seldom does this comic intuition work singly, as in "ski-nose" Bob Hope or "schnozola" Jimmy Durante. That which is straight wants to be rounded. It wishes for rotundity. According to the comic vision, this is what makes for the humor.

Dasein ist rund, said Karl Jaspers: "Existence is round!"[1] The painter Van Gogh seemed a little less assertive, but his sentiment was the same: "Life," he wrote, "is probably round."[2] La Fontaine, the fablist, confessed: "A walnut makes me quite round."[3] And Michelet, the theologian, thought "a bird to be almost completely spherical."[4] These sayings seem to follow in the spirit of the meaning of the clown's nose. Rounding takes the edge off. But it is not only rounding that is at stake in the image of the clown's face. It is a rounding *of that which is straight.* A poem by Rainer Maria Rilke captures the sense:

Tree always in the center
Of all that surrounds it
Tree feasting on
Heaven's great dome.

One day it will see God
And so, to be sure,
It develops its being in roundness
And holds out ripe arms to Him.

Tree that perhaps
Thinks innerly
Tree that dominates self.[5]

The function of rounding is also captured by Wallace Stevens:

I placed a jar in Tennessee,
And round it was, upon a hill.
It made the clovenly wilderness
Surround that hill.[6]

These poets, like the clown, suggest that roundness without straightness would result in an aesthetic or a self lacking in body, without edge or what we earlier called "gustiness." They imply that in order to "round out a rude aesthetic," giving it "inner" soul-sense, one might even look for the roundness precisely where things are straight, at the edge, in the nose.

Plato makes a similar point in his work, *The Phaedo,* when he writes: "The way to the other world is not, as Aeschylus says in the *Telephus,* . . . a straight path. If that were so, no guide would be needed, for no one could miss it; but there are many partings of the road, and windings, as I infer," Plato's Socrates says, "from the rites and sacrifices that are offered to the gods below in places where three ways meet on earth." [7] Similarly, C. G. Jung wrote concerning the soul-process that it is "made up, unfortunately, of fateful detours and wrong turnings. It is a *longissima via,* not straight but snakelike, a path that unites opposites in the manner of the guiding caduceus, a path whose labyrinthine twists and turns are not lacking in terrors." [8] Presumably these are the terrors which are like the "smashed nose" of which Sterne wrote and about which the clown knows all too well.

Were one to connect this perspective of the clown with the person and the work of Christ, there might be some modifications in the preconceptions of salvation, or of health or therapy. This perspective puts us onto the scent, perhaps even the stink, as it were, of a grace that is never cheap, but one that is purchased always at a cost. The clown cannot promise, as ego often would like to fantasize, that the "crooked shall be made straight, and the rough places a plain" (Isaiah 40:4). Christ, in his iconographic image as clown, seems rather more to the point of the saying in Ecclesiastes 1:15: "What is crooked cannot be made straight." The point seems to place the locus of religious meaning near to the deep physical carnality and violence of which myth tells, finding a sense for soul's meaning in just those moments of life when what seemed straight becomes crooked and what formerly seemed plain becomes rough for us.

The clown's nose throws a curve. It suggests that we look for passionate and erotic sense by perceiving erect and phallic straightness as a softly flaccid rounding. Find warmth where it is chilly or chilling; discover fire in life's moist messes. It is an intuition expressed poetically by Delmore Schwartz:

> *the supple recognition*
> *of the fullness and the fatness and the roundness*
> *of ripeness*
> . . . .
> *the knowledge of the ripening apple*
> *when it moves to the*
> *fullness of the time of falling to rottenness*
> *and death.*[9]

It is no wonder that the Zen (Ch'an) masters of the "shouting and beating school," during the T'ang Dynasty, are said to have tweaked the *noses* of the monks, doubtless rounding and reddening them. They did this when a monk thought or felt for a moment that he had at last attained blissful enlightenment!

17 THE RED AND THE WHITE: A CLOWN'S NASAL ALCHEMY

THERE have been many images in this meditation on Christ and the face of the clown. But what might one imagine is *really* being meant? What is the point? So what?

It began with a poem by Stevens in which smell was a metaphor of the inward journey. This beginning signalled a reversion into some strangely comic self. It occasioned a Nietzschean nostalgia for more aroma in thinking, together with a fear that we might have lost our sense of life's smell. Hans Schnier helped. But his telenose was bought at the price of drunkenness, a sort of ego-nothingness in the clown. Even so, Schnier's nose was matched by a tradition stretching from East to West in space, and from Silenos to modern Hollywood in time. It is a tradition of clowns whose perspective and whose sense of life is given image in their make-up: the round, red nose on the white face.

This nose was, as it were, seen to carry a psychology of

pathology (Fliess), of sexuality (Fenichel), and of intuition (Von Franz), all of which were expressed with feeling in Joyce's punning jokes, in Sterne's phallic humor, and in Gogol's grotesque fantasy.

In turn, these literary senses were deepened radically through myth's stories, when Greek and Indian tales located them in the violence of ego-death and in the moistening of phallic drunkenness. These were seen as ways of knowing the gods.

Between the ancient myths and modern literature there were the traditional practices of religion concerning the use of incense and its legends concerning the odor of sainthood. By viewing these religious motifs against a mythological background and as played out in literary perspectives about life, a "new" iconography of Christ was sensed, connecting His person and work with that of the clown.

A part of this work was seen to be like that of the literal nose on our faces: a moistening and warming of our airs. These literal functions were, in the last two chapters, psychologized so that the nasal imagination was likened to the appropriateness of expressing our various deep experiences through common sense, fantasy, imagination, memory, and conjecture, along with sensing soul's meaning in precisely those crooked, curvy, rounded places in life where straight and up-right seem no longer quite to the point.

So the story has gone. But what does it mean?

How could anyone know? Surely such knowledge would itself be conjecture, intuition, fantasy, or perhaps a bit of wit. Knowing what it all really means would require, in the case of the clown and Christ, nothing less than our very souls and bodies, our psyche and its eros, the life of our own death.

Such knowing would have to ask: When do we, in actual fact, experience moisture?—in depression, in the many varieties of our tears, in an affair of sex, in alcoholic stupor, in the fluid knees and elbows of athletic exhaustion, in sweat of all sorts, in grief, in diarhhea, in soupy sentimentalism, in the post-nasal drip of some sickness, and in all our many drownings: in blood, in phlegm, in choleric bile, and in saturnic dark?

But that is not all. One would also need to ask: When is our straightness warmly rounded, the square corners not so square, the edge taken off?—in a joke's momentary laughter, a child's smile, in fantasies of feared insanity, in dream, in the intimacy of a forbidden friend, in mad moments of immorality, in church's sacrament or mystic's meditation, in therapy?

In such real and literal moistenings and warmings as these we might now begin to suspect and even look for the figure of some inner clown, a clod, a fool, a violent Christ. We might in this way discover a clown's face lurking in our circus' rings, something ringing true. And that ruddy fool might be asked what he smells. What do these moistures and warmings of my life smell like? There may be soul's intuition waiting for us in these passions: something rude and real, but not quite literal. Some odor!

There is something else here, too. There are moments when some figure deep within is caught by an image of the literal nose: an adolescent girl staring at the mirror and sobbing self-consciously about the size or shape of her nose; a matron's request for a plastic surgeon's art, for a nose-job; or a sense of ethnic self-consciousness in the nose's shape; perhaps a tic in the left nostril that will not leave me alone; or dreams and day-dreams about the odd nose, its pimples, its drips, its being blown and its not being able to be cleared of stuffiness.

Instead of being overcome by these literal noses, taking them at face value, as we like to say, one now might begin to see the complex of it all. Instead of being cured of our noses, we might allow the images we have of their "wrongness" to be already a revelation. Perhaps we could begin to sense in these actual fears and real anxieties, in these frustrations and guilts, these compensations and their shame, something else, a little less literal, perhaps a bit of divinity, grotesque gods and goddesses, a clown-*daimon* here or there. Could there be in these emotions and moods of nasality a psychic moistening of soul's dryness, a dampening of our ego-airs? Could this sensing be a source of warmth to us, a sort of candle-flame in the face? Could it become our body's intuition of soul's meaning? Something smelled!

If so, it would be a curious alchemy, this transformation of literal and metaphoric, of body and soul. We might think of it as the alchemy of red and white, having something to do with "make-up."

It is not for nothing that those Naiads painted elderberry juice on Silenos' face before he taught them about the gods. Nor is it accidental that mystics spoke of Christ as white rose and red, or as lily and red-bud. Fairy tales, too, tell of Snow White in relation to Rose Red, and of Sleeping Beauty whose white skin bled drops of red blood. Even St. Bernard's mother, while pregnant with the one who was to become a saint, dreamed of a white dog with a red back, as if this were a religious image prefiguring in color what was to come.[1]

There is in the tradition of alchemy a language to speak about all this.[2] The alchemists observed that a curious redness which they called *rubedo* sometimes came into the *prima materia* after it had become white, or as they said, after *albedo*. The process could take different forms. It might be a sulfuric red in the midst of the white of mercury, as if there were a bit of passion or anger which comes into the mercurial twistings and turnings of self. Or it might take the form of a so-called "wedding" between *solis et lunae*, between "sun and moon," as if there were some fire or a spark of warmth which accompanies lunacy. It might even show itself as a connection between the white of saltiness and the red of a sulfuric anger, as if these belong together.

But whatever form it would take, the whitening (*albedo* or

leukosis) was observed to come as a result of a separation, a division, a mortification, or a calcificating dryness. This serves, curiously, to release some red, called *anima* or "soul."³ Jung quotes an old text about this, the *Oposculum agnoris ignoti:* "The stone is first an old man and then a youth, because the albedo comes at the beginning and the rubedo at the end."⁴

But the end is joined together with the beginning in the clown's face. The red is in the white. When the matters of life go "white," as alchemist and clown both seem to sense, an important process is about to be undertaken. If the temperature is raised (the alchemist's advice) or the understanding is deepened comically (the clown's urging not to see it literally), there may appear in the *tincturus albeda* or in the *lapidus albus*, in the "white tincture or rock," a rounded warmth, a moistened intoxication, a spot of red.⁵

About this spot. Nietzsche's Zarathustra asked:

> Do you not smell it? A smell is secretly welling up, a fragrance
> and smell of eternity, a rose-blessed, brown cold-wine fragrance
> of old happiness, of the drunken happiness of dying at midnight,
> that sings: the world is deep, *deeper than day had been aware.*⁶

Perhaps the point is plain as the nose on the face of the deep. Facing the clown within helps us to expect that—grotesquely, erotically, physically, sensually, mortally, painfully, violently, and passionately—things may well go white in our lives. But if we were to stay with that white, whatever it may be, facing it firmly, as it were, then we might begin to sense in that very experience a little round redness surfacing out of the depths: as if, in the middle of the white, there were a small sunrise!

It was just this sunrise which the prophet, Malachi, referred to as the Messiah, saying: "The sun shall rise with healing in its wings!"⁷ Christ the Sun!—the red nose on death's white face of the clown!

PART THREE

CHRIST, THE GREAT TEACHER

18 FULLNESS AND TIME

No CHRISTOLOGICAL meditation is complete without a consideration of a sense of time and timing. The very idea of a Christ is ineluctably connected to time and timing: God was in Christ in time; the Word became flesh; the In-finite was Incarnate; the Lord entered history; the Messiah has come. "Redeem the time," said the poet W. H. Auden in his Christmas oratorio. Time is indeed the problem for which—or so the Christian believes—Christ is the answer. But what does all this mean?

In a Christian scheme of things the key to "time" (*kairos*) is "fullness" (*plēroma*). The crucial scripture is in Mark 1:15: *peplērōtai ho kairos*, "the time is fulfilled." The idea seems to be that when "time" is "filled," important things happen; and when there is some authentic happening, we may be assured that "time" is then "full" or "filling."

Were one to follow this Christian fantasy seriously, one might say that when "time" is "filled," grapes ripen, education occurs, there may be a wedding or an important relationship, a child is born, a loved one dies, there is a break-down or a break-through, one moves to a new home or job, and so on.

One might also say this the other way around: namely, that whenever these things happen, not to mention other events like them, then "time" is "filled," then there is "good news," "gospel" (*kērygma*), "good *spiel*," some Kingdom is "at hand." There is then a "turning" (*metanoeite*), some new fidelity in life. But the key to understanding it, or so Jesus was said by Mark to say, is some sense of "fulness" (*plēroma*).

There is power and fullness in the very language with which the Gospel-writer reports this. Not only does *kairos*, the Scripture's term for "time," indicate a temporal *quality*, rather than some *quantity* (for which the word in Greek would have been *chronos*); but the language also carries in its various uses an indication of the *sort* of quality which "kairotic" times are sensed to have. For the Greeks, *plēroma* could mean being filled, for example, with "excrement" (Oribasius),[1] with "passion" (Plutarch),[2] with "years" that make one old (Herodotus),[3] with a "foetus" (Aristotle),[4] with too much breath (Aeschylus)[5] or a glut of rage (Sophocles, Euripides).[6] Especially, however, the word *plēroma* was used to refer to the sensual satisfaction of being gorged with food or drink. There are examples of this in the dialogue *Gorgias* by Plato,[7] and in Euripides' plays (for instance, *The Cyclops, Ion,* and *Iphigenia at Taurus*).[8]

This suggests that *plēroma* is a particular kind of "filling." It is always concrete and its concreteness connects with the body. One might conclude that any theology of "time" which lacks in body's sense, in carnal concreteness, or in particularity, is somehow missing the soul of a Christian notion of *kairos*, of "time." Lose body, lose Christian soul. Customary theological abstractions and spiritual airs of piety will not do.

Just here lies the problem with the imaginal world of teaching, that is, with images of teacherly incarnations. It was in "the fullness of time," in one of those moments of time's being filled, that Jesus came and was experienced by some to be a Messiah, a Christ. Not only was he experienced as Messiah and Christ, but he also was addressed directly as "Teacher," as one can see from more than two-dozen such references in Scripture.[9] In Mark and Luke he is even referred to as the Good or Great Teacher (*didaskale agathe*).[10] Justin Martyr, the early Christian thinker, wrote in his work, *The Apology:* "Our teacher is . . . Jesus Christ."[11] It would seem from this that when "time" is "full," teaching or learning is one of the things that may be happening. And when true (Good or Great) teaching happens, "time" is "full." For the Christian believer, the incarnate Christ who came in "time's fullness" is a primary image of the Teacher.

All this seems straight-forward enough. So what is the problem?

The problem has already been hinted at: it is a matter of imagination. On the one hand, if, in the Christian culture of the West, consciously or unconsciously, the image of all teaching and all teachers is christianized, religified, and spiritualized by suggestions that *true* teachers are really little christs, *imitatio christi*, "imitations of a religious ideal," then the scholarly fantasy of teaching unwittingly becomes rarified and idealized. This may function to remove it from the common experiences we have of teaching and learning which may be not so spiritual. On the other hand, if Jesus of Nazareth is viewed didactically and pedagogically through the well-polished lens of a Western scholastic tradition, a lens that has been fashioned in the knowledge-mills of academe, then religion could come to be thought of as a sort of think-tank operation in which the Gospel and religious meaning is viewed as information. This is, of course, a long way from theology's deepest hope. In both cases the body of soul, whether in religion or in education, is lost.

This could be put another way. On the one hand, thinking, education, and teaching lack a sense of feeling, a sort of Pascalian heart of reason. On the other hand, christology, not to mention other theological notions, miss the real sense of everyday life, that sensual gorging likened by the Gospel's language to food and drink, to mood and passion. Teaching in such instances has no timing, no *kairos*. Fullness is absent from thinking. Certainly it would be ironic were the Christian theological idea of "time's fullness" lacking in the very liveliness it teaches, a teaching of Christ the Teacher whose coming signals "time's being filled."

It is a problem, indeed. It is a problem for those who are religious and for those who are non-religious. It is a conundrum for a theology of Christ the Teacher and for a way of thinking and feeling any teacher's teaching. The issue becomes timely, and crucially so, whenever either religion or education seems less than full.

The reflections in the chapters which follow come from the context of this problem. They are one attempt to recover by way of imagination a plerotic *kairos*, a full timing that may well lurk deeply in the images of the Great Teacher. That such body and soul indeed abide in that imaginal world is the intuition of faith's fantasy when it says *peplērōtai ho kairos,* "the time is fulfilled"!

19 TEACHING/PREACHING: AN INSIDE/OUTSIDE SPLIT

FROM time to time the Western theological imagination becomes adamantly articulate about the teaching of Jesus whom it has called the Great Teacher. It argues—curiously—that it is not teaching at all! Rather, it is called preaching.

J. N. Sanders, in 1952, summarized two millenia of theological ideas on this matter. He wrote: "The writers of the New Testament draw a clear distinction between teaching, *didachē*, and preaching, *kērygma*, . . . The fundamental activity of Jesus . . . can be described . . . as *evangelion* and *kērygma*." [1] Luther had already made the point by distinguishing the notions of *Prediger* ("preacher") and *Lehrer* ("teacher"), as had Calvin in separating Jesus' work of *prêcher* and *enseigner*. Emil Brunner, a well-respected Protestant theologian of our time, put the point even more forcefully with the following words:

> The historical appearance of Jesus was primarily that of a Jewish rabbi, a Teacher of *Torah* . . . But *is* He really a Rabbi? . . . It is

111

. . . not true that Jesus was a Rabbi. For He does not speak about the Law of which Rabbis speak. He does not speak about truths at all. He witnesses to a reality, namely, the coming Kingdom of God.[2]

This is to say that Jesus is a preacher and not *primarily* a teacher. It is a point on which, in spite of their fundamental theological difference, Karl Barth and Emil Brunner agree. In fact, in our time it is surely Barth, beyond all others, who is compelled to make this point an issue. Barth writes: ". . . instruction . . . cannot as such pretend to be proclamation (preaching). As such, instruction . . . has to teach, . . . and to that extent not to proclaim." Then Barth adds decisively that preaching and not teaching "is in direct touch with God."[3]

To be sure, there have been theologies different from that of this *kerygmatic*, Pauline-Barthian fantasy. The Liberal Theology of the nineteenth century stressed the notion of Jesus as Teacher, a notion which, in part, Barth and Brunner were attempting to correct in the names of Luther and Calvin, not to mention that of Scripture. This correcting of a tradition that would emphasize Jesus the Teacher takes on the tone of a hunt for heresy. The testifying to the primacy of preaching over teaching fears a crypto-Pelagianism in theology's liberal mood, that is, a stress on salvation by education, by instruction, by human effort, by reason and by will. Orthodox theology attests to another mediation: namely, to grace, especially in matters of life's deepest meaning, in matter's of time's filling. Further, it tends to see no divine grace in *human* teaching. Some things cannot be taught, it seems to say.

Indeed, the history of Occidental theology—its swinging back and forth between heresy and orthodoxy, between Augustine and Aquinas, between conservative and liberal, between modernist and fundamentalist—all this could be traced by noting whether teaching or preaching in religious matters is taken as more primary. Yet there is a convergence in these antagonisms, in this endless internecine warfare in theology. The antagonists agree on one thing: on the fantasy that preaching and teaching are distinct, that they do not go together, and that one is superior to the other.

There is even some Scriptural basis for this split, as if the back-and-forth were an issue from the start. The passage already cited from Mark's Gospel in the last chapter is to the point. When the "time is fulfilled," the Gospel writer says, "Jesus came into Galilee, preaching (*kerussōn*) the gospel of God." [4] It does not say that the gospel is taught. Likewise, in Matthew's account, when Jesus commissions the disciples, they are to preach the Kingdom, not to teach it.[5] So, in spite of the numerous times that Jesus is referred to as Teacher in the Scripture, it is in fact the case that preaching and proclamation seem favored as descriptions of His work.[6] Indeed, there is specific effort, especially by Matthew and Paul, to distinguish Jesus' ministry from those who taught, that is, the Rabbis, and particularly to separate it from the teaching of the Scribes and Pharisees. Matthew and Mark put it succinctly: "He taught as one who had authority, and not as their scribes." [7]

All this may seem an academic, theological debate, an esoteric quibble of religious thinkers. But such is not the case. Like so many theological notions, this one creeps unawares, as if on its own, into secular ways of sensing life. For example, we enter unwittingly the arena of this dispute each time we suspect that the intellectualistic university professor is inferior to the one who "really" expresses feeling, to one who is willing to deal with, to name, and to confess experience in the so-called "real world."

The Western theological tendency which splits teaching off from preaching has long cultural expression, and the fact that this expression begins prior to the writing of the Christian Bible suggests that theologians may have picked up some universal schizophrenia of the soul and baptized it with spiritual sanction, giving men and women everywhere religious reason for imagining that the teacher is inferior, a rationale for supposing that professorial sorts of persons of whatever vocation are lacking in real soul and real body. Direct touch—this fantasy feels—is in proclaiming, in testifying to what is personally appealing, confessing the lords and saviors of everyday experiences. We all know well this way of seeing and feeling, both about others and about ourselves.

Aristophanes caricatured the attitude. His socratic teacher is pictured with head in the clouds and his feet not on the ground. This Greek comedian's Socrates lacks in body and in soul, being made of the cloudy, airy *spiritus,* of rationality and rationalization. It is an old image of the absent-minded pedagogue which became so common that it was used as a stock mask in Greek and Roman comedy.

The picture is that of an ivory-towered teacher who uses private language, foreign terminology, words of too many unneeded syllables, intentionally obfuscating, hardly knowing what he himself is saying, employing mind rather than heart, naming myriads of dead persons appropriately boxed and buried in footnotes, totally lacking in common sense, silly in his own condescensions, engaged in a "head trip," being saturninely melancholic about minutia, and forever occupied with long sentences(!).

The very Socrates who was so ridiculed by the comic poet himself aimed similar sarcasm at the sophistries of other teachers in Greece. But it did not end there. The barb was to extend to Molière's music masters and Shakespeare's tutors. Nor did it stop with classical French and English farce. In contemporary literature, Harold Pinter, in the play, *Homecoming,* has written about an impotent college teacher named Teddy. Philip Roth has given his readers a picture of a "professor of desire" who is so over-sexed as to be lacking in mind's sense. Wallace Stevens, also, has poetized about a Professor Eucalyptus, the "nincompated pedagogue" of New Haven whose name indicates a dryness not unlike that of the eucalyptus tree. The poet tells us that Eucalyptus makes interior things "exterior." [8]

It would seem that we do not much like the teacher. Both Freud and Jung said rude things about professors who are not in touch with the body of psyche and with soul's body. These old dogs will never be able to teach us new tricks!—or so popular wit has it. Indeed, there has been a good deal of this depreciating fantasy rampant through the years, hemlock a-plenty for every Socrates.

What is the meaning of this splitting-off of the teacher? There may be a clue or two in the language of theology which gives religious sanction to the split. As has already been said, it is the terms *kērygma* and *didachē* which have constellated the imaginal complex in which the distinction is insisted upon religiously. Several things may be noted about this complex of "preaching" and "teaching."

First, *kerussein*, "preaching," according to tradition, is supposed to occur in a loud voice, out loud. *Didaskein*, "teaching," on the other hand, is traditionally whispered. The ancient herald or proclaimer (Greek, *kērux;* Sanskrit, *kāru,* which means "singer" or "poet") is named from an Indoeuropean root, *qar-* or *qarā-,* meaning "to cry out loud." The word is also linked to the Old Persian, *xrausa,* and to the Modern Persian, *xuros,* which refer to the cock which cries aloud to waken the morning.[9] It was a common-place among the Greeks that the herald or "preacher" had above all to possess a good voice, being able to project it a great distance. The *Iliad* and the *Odyssey,* not to mention Aristotle and Demosthenes, make it a point of honor for the *kērux* not to use a megaphone or voice-trumpet.[10] So also in the Greek version of Hebrew Scriptures, the word *kerussein* is used in the sense of "crying out" or "sounding the alarm." Especially one finds this use among the prophets (for example, Micah 3:5; Jonah 3:2; Hosea 5:8; Isaiah 61:1; Zephanaiah 3:14; Zecharaiah 9:9; Jeremiah 20:8; *etc.*).

This loud, projected expression is contrasted with another sort of speaking, as for example in Luke's Gospel, where one reads: "Nothing is covered up that will not be revealed, or hidden that will not be known. Whatever you have said in the dark shall be heard in the light, and what you have whispered in private rooms shall be proclaimed upon the housetops."[11] Preaching here is distinguished from the dark, private whispering that goes on inside, in the synagogue, for instance. It is likened to that activity of the Rabbi, for whom it was customary not to teach in the streets but occasionally to give a word to some *kērux*, to some "herald," so that what was taught inside might be "proclaimed out loud." What was whispered in the herald's ear would be proclaimed in the streets.[12] Preaching, then, is voicing out loud; teaching is private talk, inside whisperings.

This connects to a second distinction between preaching and teaching: namely, it was customary in the Jewish world to sit down to teach and to stand up to preach. This is reflected, for example, in Luke 4:21, Matthew 5:1, and Mark 9:35.[13] Preaching is, as it were, standing up for something; teaching is sitting on it!

It is only a short step to a third distinction. We have already implied that in the Jewish context teaching was an indoor activity, in the synagogue, and therefore for insiders, whereas preaching was for outsiders, out-of-doors. So it was for the early Christians, too, that preaching (*kērygma*) was for converting non-believers, that is, outsiders, whereas teaching (*didachē*) was for instructing those who already believed. Teaching was for catechumens. It was a case of faith which already existed "seeking understanding" (*fides quaerens intellectus*). In this way teaching was thought to involve *gnosis* ("knowledge") or *intelligere* ("intellect"), whereas preaching, which on this view was thought to be primary, works by *pistis* ("faith") or *credere* ("belief").[14] That is, preaching is for all on the outside; teaching is for the few inside!

To these classical theological distinctions may be added one from popular lore. The teacher or professor is commonly imagined to be absent-minded (*agnosis*, "agnostic"). He is the man of mind who is mindless. On the other hand, the preacher is caricatured in the popular imagination as one who does not practice what he preaches. This notion is already spoken of in Matthew's Gospel. There the Pharisees are spoken of as those who preach but do not practice.[15] Were one to assume some wisdom lurking in the people's wit, some truth in this hyperbole, yet another distinction could be articulated. It would be that preaching is that which has nothing really to do with practice, with behavior, and that teaching is that which has less to do with reason and more to do with reason's absence than one might at first have thought.

Such are the discriminations between preaching and teaching which a long tradition has given us. The fantasy is well-ensconced in religious and secular worlds alike. But what can one make of it?

20 MAKING OUTER INNER: THE TWO AS ONE

AT THE end of the last chapter we used the word "fantasy" to refer to the well-ensconced popular and theological distinction between preaching and teaching. According to Robert Grant, it is fantasy indeed, however crucial it may be to imagination's long life. Grant writes:

> In previous times it was customary to contrast Jesus with Paul, or the Jesus of History with the Christ of Faith, or the synoptic gospels with the Fourth Gospel. . . . For a time there were those who believed that the essential "kerygma" could be emphasized at the expense of the less significant "didache," though the fairly obvious *fact* that in early Christianity *"gospel" included both preaching and teaching* lessens the force of this contrast. More recently it has been fashionable to compare the authentic Hebrew elements in the New Testament with the less satisfactory elements which can be called "late Jewish" or "Greek."
> The chief difficulty with these antitheses is that they are *not*

historical. They arise out of the needs of modern writers to pick and choose among various elements . . . laying emphasis on certain distinctive, or seemingly distinctive features in various documents and by *neglecting equally important resemblances.*[1]

Splitting teaching off from preaching is simply not defensible as a Biblical idea, denigrating one or elevating the other. Then from where do we get this idea which is so pervasive in Western life? The dichotomy must belong properly to some fantasy, to a complex of imagination.

The Biblical image is different, as indeed Grant notes. Jesus taught *and* preached. He did both of these in the streets *and* in the synagogue. Outsiders received his preaching and teaching, but so also did Jews. He preached while *sitting* beside a lake, and he taught standing up.[2] The main mode of speaking which Jesus used—namely, parables—was teaching and preaching *both at once.* It has often been noted by the very theologians who would like to make the distinction between *kērygma* and *didachē* that in parables such a difference between functions of paranesis and proclamation are impossible to sustain.[3] So, one might conclude that if Christ be an image of the Great Teacher, then in *great* teaching, preaching and teaching are one!

It is as if in Jesus' preaching/teaching, when "time" is "fulfilled," inside and outside are the same. In "the fullness of time," the two are together, if not one. Or, to put it another way, when the Kingdom's perspective comes near, ". . . the two (are) one, . . . the inner as the outer and the outer as the inner."[4]

Such a way of seeing may seem contrary to our natures, as well as to the fantasy which splits the two. We may prefer the split. Perhaps we do not want our preachers to teach, giving explanations, killing with a thousand qualifiers, offering little nigglings that might bring to clarity those sermonic homilies which we can keep at a distance so long as they remain rhetorically clever and oratorically cryptic. Also, it may be that we do not want our teachers to preach in the classrooms or to express themselves openly in scholarly articles or books. It may be difficult for us to get the full sense of the German idiom, *Gelehrten ist gut Predigen,* which means, "A word to the wise is sufficient," but which also says literally that good teaching is preaching and that good preaching teaches.

Nonetheless, *our* preferences and wishes aside, the Biblical tradition seems to urge against this split. It suggests perhaps that if the distinction be fantasy well-ensconced in us and in our tradition, then we might place both sides of it where it properly belongs. We might notice that it is something imagined. This neat distinction between preaching and teaching is not externally objective, existing in "outer" history and in social roles. It belongs in a deeper place. We might wish to own the inside/outside, teaching/preaching fantasy as a soul-split, a severence in the self. Perhaps then we could begin to withdraw the projection of this pathology away from tradition's history, and locate the disembodied teacher and the soul-less preacher both deeply in the self, a self well-tutored, if schizophrenically, by the archetypal image from a theological past. In this way "outer" theology is viewed as depth psychology, and the distinctions of the tradition between teaching and preaching begin to take on a new sense.

Now, the "preacher" is in the self. It is that figure within which wants to voice, to express, to say out loud, to cry loudly, to publish, to give testimony. This "preacher" within is opposed to some inner "teacher" who ruminates privately, darkly, in whispered tones, speaking with only those figures inside his own sacred life-space. The inner "teacher" is not concerned with mind at all but is, as the popular image indeed says, absent minded. Nor is behavior or practice the most important matter to the inner "preacher" who indeed seldom practices what he voices expressively. These two figures within the self are split off from each other when "time" is empty, that is, when the inner "preacher" does not care to be tutored by inner voices and when the inner "teacher" cannot manage to bring his undertoned whisperings to expression.

This splitting happens, for example, when an introverted tendency or a shyness *is viewed as* distinct from extravertish nature. The split also occurs when ethics and morality (practice, acting-out) are disconnected from spirituality and mystical moments (quietism, inner life). Or again, it is this split which manifests itself when sociological explanations are thought to be superior to psychology's solipsism and narcissism. Many other symptoms of the split will come to the reader's mind.

We suffer continually this theological fantasy in life. Our inner "preacher" fights the "teacher" in the cave of self constantly. When we voice out loud, stand up for things, see everything as external to the self, and yet refuse to be practitioners, we are living the split. When we engage and indulge our private selves, lowering our moods or life-rhythms, sitting it all down a bit, making everything an inside matter, and yet absenting ourselves from our own mindfulness, we show our "teacher" split off from our "preacher." Our confessing "preacher" professes a bit too quickly, always being too eager to speak about his fidelities and infidelities; and our professorial "teacher" confesses only within his own academish groves, rationalizing this and that and everything.

To some this way of putting things may seem a psychologizing of theology's ideas. But it is not this at all. Rather, it is a response to two facts—first, the fact that a split between preaching and teaching persists so in the collective theological and secular fantasy of the West; and, second, the fact that this split does not indeed exist in the place to which it is attributed. It is difficult not to conclude, then, that the fantasy is somehow functionally important (since it has lasted so long and dominated so strongly), and that its "real" location is in the psyche, albeit a collective psyche (since it is historically not linked to the Biblical source).

Instead of accounting for the psychic split-complex psychologically, we are taking a cue from its theological and popular manifestations, not thereby psychologizing theology, but theologizing the soul, attempting to make sense of psychic reality by using images from the religious tradition.

Perhaps the point is that if we begin to feel inferior about our inner "teacher" (the one who thinks, muses, and explains) or about our inner "preacher" (the one who voices, expresses, and puts feeling into language), we might see if we can sense a split in our selves, a crucifixion of the image of Christ the Great Teacher, some tortured schism in the inner Christ. If such a division in the self produces an inferior sense, a one-sidedness, it would take the body and the soul out of preaching and teaching, and then Mary's question before the empty tomb, following the crucifixion, becomes timely: "Where have they put the body?"

21 FROM SOCRATES TO SILENOS: REMYTHOLOGIZING THE IMAGE OF THE TEACHER

IN EARLIER chapters the futility of grounding the image of Christ the Teacher in the prototype of the Jewish Rabbi was noted. Scripture itself is concerned to contrast rather than to compare Jesus' teaching with rabbinic ways.[1] In the ancient world this leaves only Greek paradigms and models as resource.

Indeed, among the early Church Fathers, there were those who looked for the meaning of the teacher, Christ, by drawing analogy with Socrates. Clement of Alexandria, for example, proposed the phrase, *ho didaskolos,* "the teacher," as a title for the last four books of his work now known as *Stromata.* In these chapters the Alexandrian Father compares the person and work of Christ to the teaching of Greek philosophers, most notably Plato and Socrates.

This tendency to find a model for Christ the Teacher in Socrates continued in the West. In the seventeenth century, Guez de Balzac wrote a work called, *Socrate chrétian* ("Christian Socratism"). In more recent times, the movement of Christian Humanism, as well as the philosophical theologizing of Étienne Gilson, has carried on this socratizing of Christ.[2] So pervasive has this tendency been that Lee Capel, for one, refers to it as "the recurrent comparison between Socrates and Christ."[3]

Søren Kierkegaard, Karl Jaspers, and Stanley Hopper have all shown what Kierkegaard calls "the similarity," "the true analogy," between Socrates and Christ, though these three have introduced a reticence into the comparison.[4] They note that to view the Great Teacher, Christ, in the manner of Socrates may risk making religious teaching philosophical and intellectualistic rather than, as would be intended, to give soul to a Western notion of education. In this way Christ the Teacher could become humanized. Transpersonal and transcendental dimensions would tend to be obscured.

There is a latent rationalism in the Socratic image. It is a rationalism given to the Socratic image by Plato who moved the former's concern for "soul" into philosophical and metaphysical abstractions. Virtue comes to be seen as knowledge and sin is viewed as ignorance.[5] So it is that where Socrates is petitioned, the very quest for body in the soul of teaching is detoured. A christified Socrates or a socratized Christ may simply heighten the distinction between mind and body, soul and reason, love and logos, teaching and preaching. Philosophizing Christ's image may make persist the very fantasy which would be beside the point were "time" really "full."

Yet there is something lurking in the tendency to equate the teaching of Christ with that of Socrates. It is something that may be overlooked by the metaphysical and humanistic traditions. Epictetus, in his *Discourses,* spoke of a Socrates whose Great Teaching was *kērygma,* a "preaching." He spoke of this philosopher as *kērux,* as a "herald" of "good news." The teaching of Socrates was, Epictetus says, a "mission," the work of a "mediator," a "messenger of God," and it was impelled by the *daimon* of soul.[6] This way of viewing Socrates is quite different from that of philosophical humanism.

The difference has been spoken of in essays by James Hillman and Pierre Hadot. The former connects the teaching of Socrates to *eros,* to erotic love, as exemplified especially in the dialogue, *The Symposium.* It is the physical and sensual sense of connectedness (*eros*) which carries the teaching (*logos*). Hadot draws upon the same dialogue as does Hillman and stresses the Dionysian dimension of philosophical inquiry. Dionysian enthusiasm and *eros* give form to a teaching which cannot be distinguished from preaching. There is voice in the quiet whisperings of the inner soul, and there is soul in the cryings out loud. Inner is outer, and outer has a deep interiority. Soul has body, rather than airy or rationalistic spirituality. And body has some depth in soul. Such a vision of Socrates may indeed be, like that of Epictetus, an important background for an understanding of Christ the Teacher . . . if it could be not forgotten in later philosophical, theological, and educational contexts.[7]

It is Alcibiades who remembers Dionysos in Socrates' teaching. It is he who senses the *eros* of *logos,* the passion of ideas. He sees in Socrates the Teacher a *daimon,* the god Eros himself. For Alcibiades, Socrates' teaching is one with preaching. We are told of this sense of things by Alcibiades' references to mythology, as if somehow myth lay behind philosophy, being the body of its soul and meaning.

In *The Symposium,* Plato recalls Alcibiades as saying that the greatness of Socrates' philosophical teaching is that he is like the mythical god Silenos. This ugly tutor to Kings Midas and Solon, to the god Dionysos as well as many others, was represented in fat, little statuettes which, when you opened them in the middle, were empty. But the empty center was filled with little figurines, little people inside. These were images of all the gods and goddesses. The silenic emptiness was full of divinity. So Socrates' person and his teaching words were like Silenoi . . . or so said Alcibiades.[8]

If "christian socratism" leads from theology's image of the Great Teacher back to Greek philosophy, then Plato's *Symposium* suggests yet another step. The Occidental fantasies of teaching which go behind Christ to Socrates imply beneath Socrates the figure of Silenos. Behind Christian theology may be the forms of thinking from Greek philosophy; but beneath philosophy are all the gods and goddesses of Greek myth.

To be sure, there are many mythic images of the Great Teacher which might give substance to a view of Christ. Justin Martyr, speaking precisely of Christ the Teacher, names some possibilities: Mercury, who like Christ is the messenger of God to man; Asculapius, who is the one wounded for man and is himself a healer; Hercules, who suffered but taught a heroic way; Bacchus, who instructed men about the transformation of water and wine; Ariadne, who showed a labyrinthine way; Perseus; Bellerophon; and the Dioscuri.[9] There are also other archetypal teachers in this tradition: Artemis, who taught the hunt; Demeter, who taught men how to till and nourish; Prometheus, who taught how to light the fire and how to sacrifice; the Fates and Muses, who teach us everything and about whom Aristophanes says that they are *didaskaloi* ("teachers") whose poetry is *therapontēs* ("therapy").[10]

All these, and others, too, are candidates for bodying forth Christic teacherliness. Yet it is Socrates who persists in the Western imagination as the ideal, and, if we can trust drunken Alcibiades, it is Silenos who gives meaning to Socrates' mythic depths. So, for purposes of these meditations it shall be Silenos whom we petition as archetypal image of the Great Teacher, since inside his emptiness, wonderful to say, are all the other gods and goddesses![11]

22 SILENOS AND CHRIST: THE TRUE VINE AS THE GREAT TEACHER

IT IS sometimes not so easy to find the *mythos* of a truly Great Teacher. Silenos, for example, hides his real identity, being part animal, half some satyr horse, or perhaps half some goat like Pan.[1] He sleeps in a deep cave.[2] He does not publish, nor does he lecture. Yet Aelian and Virgil say he can be snared. Especially, he can be trapped into teaching using garlands of flowers, as do the Naiads. King Midas managed to obtain his teaching by making him drunk, as if the intoxication were already the appearance of some tutor or some tutelege.[3] The nymphs—that is to say, the fantasiasts, the fantasies—know where he is, as Apollodorus attests.[4] He is himself a satyr, the central character of all satyr plays. Kerényi has even gone so far as to say that the "silenic nature" is the "seat of the comic," as if great teaching were somehow ineluctably comedic.[5]

Difficult as it may be to locate Silenos in life, he nonetheless appears. He is teacher to king and fool, to lawmaker and to lawbreaker, to sober hero and to mad maenad. He instructs the gods and goddesses themselves. As the Orphic Hymn witnesses, he is honored by them all.[6] Silenos is an ithyphallic tutor, one who can teach Dionysos and Ariadne how to wed.[7] This is to say that he is a teacher's teacher. Perhaps it is just because of this fact that he was reticent to show himself, as if this quality goes with great teaching.

Yet Silenos' secret was not well hid. Two things are universally said about him by such as Pausanius, Ovid, Plutarch, Cicero, Theogonis, Bacchylides, Sophocles, Plato, and others ... though at least Plutarch mentions that it would be better were we not to know these two things about the Great Teacher's teaching.[8]

The first thing is that he was a drunk, a heavy man, saturnine. He was known to drink—or so goes the tale—for ten days and ten nights without stopping. However, the drunkenness was special in Silenos' case. It is, for example, to be distinguished from that of Dionysos, as Otto notes.[9] In order to describe Silenos' particular drunken nature, an Orphic Hymn uses a phrase that was already employed by Aeschylus, Euripides, and Plato.[10] In Greek the phrase is: *galēnioōn thiasoisin*. It refers to a "deep stillness," like the calmness deep within a stormy sea. It may well be that Silenos' riotous drunkenness, manifesting a deep rootedness, is linked to the second aspect of his secret, namely, his teaching.

Silenos taught—to use Plutarch's words—that "the best thing for all men and women is not to be born. However, the next best thing to this, and the first of those to which man can really attain, is, after being born, to die as quickly as possible." [11] Rhode cites ancient fragments which tell that it would be second best, according to Silenos, to return to "Night" (*nuktos*) or to Hades' place of soul (*thalamos*).[12] Similarly, an Orphic Hymn says of Silenos' orgiastic teaching that it took place at night (*orgia nuktiphan*).[13]

What is this going into night's darkness, into death, that constitutes the wise teaching of Silenos? While musing this question let us keep in mind that it is an intoxicated mythic fantasy. It could be important to keep its "logic" in that realm, that is, in Silenos' cave, in the metaphors of myth. Perhaps it is not a physical, literal death that is meant, but rather an acknowledging of all dyings, all that occur when ego is born, and a dying which being born may require of us.

This way of sensing Silenos' preaching/teaching could open a veritable *plēroma* of life's timing, as in the case pointed to by Kerényi where Silenos is the cause of a gain in soul through the ego-dying experienced in an initiation rite. The particular instance is a Porto sarcophagus where Silenos is depicted as offering a young male initiate a butterfly, the Greek word for which is also the term meaning "soul" (*psychē*).[14] Silenos is giving "soul," but the initiate has to die (sarcophagus) to his earlier ego-life, his childishness.

The dying away of perspectives of ego is likewise intimated by Silenos' intoxication. In drunkenness certain inhibitions of *persona*, the personal ego-roles, fall into moist oblivion. *In vino veritas*, one says. There is truth in intoxication, as if some deeper learning may be experienced in such "death." There may even be a connection between the teacher who is intoxicated and the one who is absent-minded, being absent of personal cleverness and ego's rationalizations. It would be a sort of learning letting ego go.

In all this it may be possible to begin to see why Alcibiades saw Silenos in his master, Socrates. Socrates was indeed "absent minded," but this was his wisdom. He said he knew nothing. He taught a philosophy which was, as he himself put it, a learning how to die. And he was certainly comfortable in the drunken revels of *The Symposium*, being calm on the morning after an entire night of intoxication and teaching.

Nor should it surprise us greatly that the image of drunkenness belongs with that of the Great Teacher. The Buddhist master Milarepa had a teacher, Marpa, a teacher's teacher, who was, according to legend, fat and constantly drunk.[15] In the Hindu tradition, Vāyu, the teaching messenger of the gods, was the first to drink the soma, according to Daniélou's account.[16] In the Sufi tradition, Al-ghazzali likens learning *real* religious experience to drunkenness, a quality, he says, lacking always in the teaching of theology at secondhand where experience is missing, that is, a teaching which is not at the same time a preaching.[17] In Nordic saga we are told to drink so that the stream of *Minne,* the wisdom of salvation, should not be interrupted.[18] And the Tucuna Indians of South America have a myth which teaches that when drunk with the strong beer of the gods, we may all live with them.[19] There are, of course, many other examples, but the common fantasy is that, in some sense, the Great Teacher is a drunk and that his teaching is intoxicating of others.

Yet there is an understandable reticence when it comes to Christ. Does not the New Testament teach, in the book of Titus, that it is the "false teacher" who is drunk? that the teacher of sound doctrine is temperate and not a slave to drink? that he controls himself? is grave? and lives a sober life not given to worldly passions?[20] This hardly seems a picture of a silenic teacher! Even heretical Gnostic versions of Christ as Teacher vehemently resist a shadow of Silenos, as Hans Jonas has decisely shown.[21] For example, the *Corpus Hermeticum* links wine, not to teaching, but to ignorance.[22] *The Odes of Solomon* testify to a spiritual, but not a bodily intoxication, one that comes from the water, not the wine, of the Lord's spring.[23] And the *Gospel of Truth* speaks of the man filled with Christ's teaching as one who has overcome the stupors of his drunkenness with the spirit's sobriety.[24]

These texts would surely lead one to think that it is a mistake to search in some silenic soul for the *plēroma* of Christ the Teacher, for the fullness where teaching and preaching connect in time and history. Is it indeed not a mistake? Perhaps. But perhaps, also, just the moralizing and the literalizing which denies in theology the silenic shadow in Christ is what takes the preaching-soul out of teaching body, opening thereby the way for a split between spiritual religion and intellectual theology, between soul and body, leaving Mary at an empty tomb, in time, surely, but out of it, too, not filled. Perhaps the shepherding pastoral tone of the book of Titus, though indeed being one possible interpretive fantasy in which theology can locate itself, has nonetheless the function of placing back the body of the Teacher in some unconscious cave. Something gets forgotten in the process, something overlooked, even repressed: the silenic shadow!

Kerényi put his finger squarely on this shade in theology's meaning when, in his book on Dionysos, he pointed to the Johannine passage where Jesus is said to say, "I am the true vine." [25] It would certainly have been enough for him to have said, "I am the vine." Why did he add the word "true"? Jesus was of course at home walking the Phoenician coast as far as Tyre, where there existed a well-established religion of the god of wine. Could it be that Jesus intended to identify himself mythically with images of this god, with a Dionysian and Silenic nature, claiming in contrast only to be the *true* embodiment of their soul's wisdom? Jeremiah had already said that the wine-stock of Israel had become a bastard vine, a "false" stem! [26]

Morton Smith has discovered additional evidence to Kerényi's point. He has demonstrated that the story of the transformation of water into wine at Cana of Galilee is modeled by the writer of the Gospel *word for word* on an already extant text describing the Greek-inspired festival of the wine god along the Phoenician coast.[27] Could it be that the writer of the Gospel had good reason, perhaps from Jesus himself, for imagining Christ the Teacher as like the Greek figure of the teacher who is drunk?

There is of course that important passage in *The Acts of the*

Apostles where outsiders thought the early Christians were drunk.[28] Peter protested, according to the story, that it was too early in the day to drink, being only the third hour. Yet the text refers to the eucharistic sacrament, and the entire sacramental theology of the Church imagines the central Christian experience to be that of a Great Teacher who is a vine. When he bleeds, it is wine: a sacramental intoxication! Intoxication as a sacrament!

Who is this Great Teacher sleeping deep within the caves of our tradition and of our selves, one who we are so ready to nail to a cross or to serve some hemlock, one who is the butt of 3000 years of "gallows humor"? Could our reticence in this regard be a fear of a fat little man seated deep within our souls, an intoxicating teacher who whispers to us secrets of the gods, and who is most fearsome of all because his deep wisdom cherishes for us that, as soon as possible after it is born, the ego-perspectives of our life should learn to die.

This is not an easy matter. Yet however offensive the juxtaposition of Christ and Silenos[29]—and there is no blinking the fact that drunkenness is offensive—it remains the case that the path of the meaning of Christ the Great Teacher leads, not to Jewish sources where its idea is alien, but directly to the dark cave of Silenos. There is the strong evidence of Kerényi, Smith, and the texts of the New Testament—evidence for which sooner or later, like our own fears and those of Titus, we must finally give account. And if such accounting could lead to "fullness" in "time," to pleromatic life . . .

Well, there is provocation enough in these things, in life-experience and in Scripture, to whet one's thirst, as it were, and to warrant pressing further the matter of the intoxicated Teacher, asking what it can possibly mean. If the probing be offensive, we might only hope that it be indeed as offensive as St. Paul said is the Gospel of Christ itself, which is a stumbling block to some and to others folly.[30]

23 BIBLICAL AND THEOLOGICAL DRUNKENNESS: THE CASES OF LOT AND NOAH

ST. IRENAEUS, many years ago, faced, and as certainly feared, the stumbling block of drink in relation to religious meaning. When looking for a saving figure, a teacher and a preacher of salvation, he encountered in Scripture one who is outrageously, immorally, and offensively drunk. This Church Father was forced to account for this. The figure in his case was not Silenos. It was Lot. But the conundrum is the same, and Irenaeus' meditation may be a clue as we, in this work, wrestle the matter of having found a shadow of Silenos behind the person of Christ the Teacher.

The question for Irenaeus was: How could a righteous man, such as Lot, one who had resisted all the evil of Sodom and Gomorrah, become drunk and lie down incestuously with his own daughters? Especially, how could Holy Scripture make of him a spiritual hero for this? Irenaeus responds:

133

> We should not hastily impute as crimes to the men of old times those actions which the Scripture itself has not condemned, but should rather seek in them types of things to come.[1]

The point here—a point Origen also made with regard to Lot—is that rather than reading literalistically and moralistically, that is, behaviorally, we might look at the Biblical text as type or archetype, as a metaphor or image. Origen, for example, suggested that the reason Celsus had thought Lot's drunkenness a crime "worse than the crimes of Thyestes" who ate his children is that Celsus did not see the figurative sense, the fantasy of the Scripture's imaginal world.[2]

Origen goes even further. He seeks the meaning of the drunkenness not only in Lot but also in Noah. How is it—he asked—that the hero of the Flood has become identified as the teacher of viniculture? And why is he depicted by Scripture as a drunk?[3] Even more curious, why are rabbinic sages, the *Zohar*, and other Church Fathers so quick to defend Noah as a "just man and perfect in his generations"?[4]

The argument of the theologians of the early Church is succinct. Noah, first, and Lot, later, are great teachers of Israel. They are ones, according to the story, on whom the on-going life of the people quite literally depends. They live in the time of the emptying of the world in the Flood and in the destruction of Sodom and Gomorrah. Sexual potency is crucial to the future of God's people. Both of these men were old, having survived a great deal. In the ancient world wine and fertility were linked. So it was the cultivation of the vine and the drinking of wine which brought a drunkenness which made eros possible, especially an intoxication which would promote an intercourse forbidden in conventional moralistic terms, but which was crucial for a continuity in religious meaning that transcends and is deeper than any moralism.[5]

Origen and Irenaeus, each in his own way, connect Lot and Noah with Christ precisely at the point of a life which comes from the vine and its fruit. Their imaginal way of theologizing "reasons" in the following manner. The two daughters who slept with Lot symbolize the Old and New Testaments, according to Origen, or the Jews and the Gentiles, according to Irenaeus. These daughters have one Father, and it is only the Father who can make the daughters fruitful and full. Semen in these accounts corresponds to soul, and both semen and soul are granted by wine's intoxication, whether in sex or in sacrament.[6] So the Church Fathers can say that Christ is like Lot and Noah. He came, as it is written in Matthew, "eating and drinking."[7] Christ is therefore a second Noah and a second Lot, responsible for the life which comes from the true vine.[8] It is in this way that one may understand the Third Gospel, when it says:

> As it was in the days of Noah, so will it be in the days of the Son of Man. They ate, they drank, they married, they were given in marriage until the day when Noah entered the ark, and the flood came and destroyed them all. Likewise as it was in the days of Lot—they ate, they drank, they bought, they sold, they planted, they built, but on the day when Lot went out from Sodom fire and brimstone rained from heaven and destroyed them all—so will it be on the day when the Son of Man is revealed. (Luke 17:26–30)

This way of viewing drunkenness is not uncommon in the ancient world.[9] For example, the term for "drunkenness" (methē or methuē) is used figuratively by Chrysostom to signify Abraham's intoxicated devotion to God even in the crime of sacrificing his son.[10] Origen, Eusebius, Dionysius the Areopagite, Gregory of Nyssa, and Cyril of Jerusalem all use the term methē ("drunk") to refer to a mystical or sacramental state of divine wisdom.[11] Philo, too, speaks of "drinking" as a cause of religious ecstasy.[12] Plotinus, in The Enneads, uses the word in a similar manner, linking his meaning of "mystical enthusiasm" to Plato's work in The Phaedo and in The Symposium.[13] Plato had himself, in both The Republic and in The Laws, viewed "drinking" (methuō) as important to education, that is, as a means of teaching and learning the kindling of emotion, a reliance on the wisdom of the nectar of the gods, rather than on mere human opinion.[14]

The Greek term used by all these writers connects with the story of Noah, where drunkenness corresponds to a flood of water. Noah is preserved from the water and is inundated by the moisture of the wine. Cyril of Alexandria hints at this association when he speaks of the Promised Land as the place which is "drunk" with good things, by which he means that it is "flooded" with them.[15] The Septuagint uses this same word for "drunkenness" to speak of rain or moisture, as for example, in Isaiah and in Psalms.[16] Wyclife's Bible made the same connection when it translated a Psalm to read: "Thou hast visited the earth and made it drunk." Jeremiah, too, notes this meaning of "drunkenness," but this prophet takes it out of the atmosphere above and places it in the soul below. So we read, in the Septuagint, *methussō tēn psychēn*, meaning "to refresh or make drunk the psyche or soul."[17] *Methē*, like many words for inebriation in the variety of the world's languages, carries at bottom the image simply of "moistening" or "making wet."

Perhaps the point is coming clearer. The so-called "drunkenness" of Lot and Noah, that which guarantees the body politic of the Hebrew people, the wine of sex, the intoxication of mystical and sacramental experience, the nectar of teaching, the inebriate depths of religious meaning that from a social and moral point of view may seem grotesque and criminal—all these have to do with "moistening." The experience of drunkenness is literal and physical. It is offensive, to be sure. Yet its very offense may indicate something deeper, namely, the moistening that signals a life of soul in the body of a people or of an individual.

There is risk in this understanding, however. It is the risk that the point of the offensive power of the silenic teaching may become lost in an allegorizing, spiritualizing tradition—in the Church's Fathers, Scripture, Philo, Plato, and Plotinus. These make the moisture of drunkenness a refreshing rain or a baptismal font. But Silenos is radical and not pretty or pious at all. One is reminded of Heraclitus' saying, "It is death for soul to become water."[18] Lot and Noah, at least, know that one can really, even if not literally, drown in that water. There is a flood in the soul from time to time!

There seem to be two mistaken paths which lead away from rather than into the silenic wisdom. First, it would be unrealistic to deny drunkenness as real and important to Silenos' teaching, as if inundation did not happen in life, those tidal wavings of time's rhythms, the diseases of tears and terrors and other fluxing humors. But second, it is also, perhaps, mistaken to invite the drunkenness, as if the moistening were some happy and sweet spiritual boon rather than the horror that it really is.

It might be put this way: the teetotaler and the alcoholic make the *same* mistake! They are both intemperately temperate in their literalism. Neither is drunk in Silenos' radical sense. The American comedian W. C. Fields made the point with wit when he remarked, "I'm not an alcoholic; I'm a drunk." It is unimaginable to say of the god Silenos, or of the pious Lot or Noah, that they are alcoholics, as unimaginable as saying that they are teetotalers. To say "alcoholic" is to make a mythic point medical or sociological. It makes a theological idea anthropological. A depth psychological insight becomes behavioral.

Unlike Silenos, Lot, and Noah—who are drunks!—the alcoholic is, paradoxically, a teetotaler. He suffers the intoxication of the literalist, Apollo, rather than that of Silenos' student, Dionysos. He thinks the only way to get drunk is to drink. The teetotaler is with Pentheus up a tree while the alcoholic is with panicked Agave attempting hysterically to be moist. Both treat Dionysos as some Lydian foreigner. One too much welcomes him, as if he did not already belong; the other uses the same fantasy to deny him.

If life is not seeming drunk, the alcoholic drinks. If life is too drunk, the teetotaler abstains. Theirs is a balancing act, a compensation, attempting to correct pathology's experiences with opposite behaviors. Mistaking ego-control for depth's autonomous soul, they think like is cured by unlike, fighting fire with water and water with fire, missing somehow the point that there is love, not war, between these two, preaching's hell-fire and teaching's aqua-vita, a fire-water of silenic drunken eros in the depths. In their fundamentalisms they both miss Silenos. To drink or not to drink is not the question. So what is?

Philo speaks to the question indirectly when writing about Moses' spring. He had already written a treatise about drunkenness and sobriety in which he had coined the phrase, *metheseōs psychēs aitia gignetai*, meaning "the drinking by which soul is led to itself." [19] Then he had described this state of psyche being led to itself as *nēphalios methē*, a "sober drunkenness." [20] The Church Father Cyril of Jerusalem had used this phrase in the same way.[21] What is this "sober drunkenness"? Is it some trick with words? some spiritual paradox? some rhetorical softening of Silenos' offensiveness? some cryptic way of getting body into spirit without achieving anything really in soul? Perhaps. But perhaps, also, it has a more forthright, experiential meaning, something a bit more obvious and less esoteric.

"Sober drunkenness" could signify a sobering of ego in the face of the experience of being filled, moistened, or drunkened in a deeper sense of self. Is it not precisely in the deepening of self that so-called "ego" is deprived of its various personal pseudo-intoxications—its pride, its opinions about this and that and everything, its thoughts and feelings? Is it not this that Silenos means when he teaches that as soon as possible after being born ego should die? The deep and radical drunken moistening of self sobers ego and its perspectives. It is an experience of sober drunkenness, of the drunkenness which sobers one. Did not the text say of Silenos' orgies that there was in them a "deep calm" (*galēnioōn thiasoisin*)?

The behaviors of ego, the "shoulds" and "oughts" of drinking or of not drinking, the "therefores" and "becauses," are all beside this point. Alcoholism *and* abstinence are both the same disease . . . from the silenic perspective. They are *theological* ailments in which one suffers a literalism. They are personal neuroses masquerading as deep pathology, social roles parading as spirited meaning. They see well the problem of "time" and its being "full" or "empty," but they view this problem to be a concern of will and reason, a matter of personal control. They view myth and religion, deep human meaning, as morality and metaphysics. They attempt to give preaching power, and teaching passion, by doing something (drinking) or by not doing (abstinence).

In the "full" moment, "time" is itself drunk, not some person. The personal perspective, whether it be sober or drunk, is considerably sobered in the "fullness of time." As *persona* (mask, or social role) gets moistened, flooded, or drowned in life, feeling deepens. An inner voice begins to speak. Images come. Thinking becomes expressive. Behavior is seen as symbolic or imaginal. Sobered are behavioral psychologies and ideological sociologies. Sobered, too, are literalistic religion and rationalistic theology. Everything begins to flow, it all being moistened. No wonder drunkenness is offensive and fearsome to ego. With the loss of the literal, everything becomes an image of soul's depth. As Goethe wrote at the end of *Faust:* "Everything that flows / Is just a metaphor." [22]

24 THE POETRY OF DRUNKENNESS

WHEN life goes drunk things seem transitory in the extreme, flowing here and there, like time's Heraclitean river. When transitory, all moves. Everything is a metaphor of something else. Images are in flux; they are flexible in their meanings. They fill us, like a veritible *plēroma*, disclosing the multifaceted, moving nature of the kairotic time we live from day to day. Time's quantity takes on imaginal quality.

Poets are at home in the *plēroma* of such non-literal moments of "time." It is therefore to them that we turn for insight into Silenos' damp cave, his teaching about death and dying, and how it all relates to Christ the Teacher.

Gerard Manley Hopkins, in a late sonnet having to do with what he calls "time's eunuch," prays: "O thou Lord of life, send my roots rain." [1] And Rainer Maria Rilke writes: "Say to the still earth: I flow. / And announce to the rushing water: I am." [2]

In these lines of Hopkins and Rilke the "water" is already something more than water. It is more like the drink of which John Milton wrote: "As with new Wine intoxicated both / They swim in mirth, and fansie that they feel / Divinitie within."[3] In the art of poetry, as Delmore Schwartz has observed, the moisture is changed. Schwartz writes: "It transforms the water into wine at each marriage in Cana of Galilee."[4] Martin Heidegger puts the matter similarly concerning a poem by Friedrich Hölderlin: "Drunkenness amplifies into a luminous clarity in which the depth of that which is hidden opens itself up and shadow appears as the sister of clarity."[5]

In poetry the water has fire. When the moistening has warmth or when the flame makes life drunkenly moist, a poetizing is happening, a making of meaning. The clue to poetry's metaphors of drunkenness is in the phrase "fire water." "Fire" and "water" are separately images which indicate, from time to time, how we sense ourselves: on the one hand, fiery, and on the other, dissolving. But "fire water" implies a special experience, those moments when these two usually discrete and even opposite senses somehow occur together, phosphorescently, as it were.[6]

Gaston Bachelard makes this point by distinguishing the imagery of "water" in the writings of Edgar Allan Poe and in that of E. T. A. Hoffmann. Poe's poetic reverie has to do with "heavy water" (*l'eau lourde*). It is an imagery of "filling the depths" (*la profondeur pleine*). "Times that are past are a deep water for our soul." Poe, like Heraclitus, connects fluid metaphors to passing time and death. "This is the lesson," Bachelard writes; "it is a death in depth, a death which lives with us daily, near to us, in us."[7] That is to say, the lesson of "water" is a dying of and to soul.

Though moistening was a deepening for Poe, and heavily so, his water had no fire. Bachelard says:

Edgar Allan Poe was truly without hearth . . . Alcohol did not warm him, comfort him, or make him gay! Poe never danced around a blazing punch bowl like a human flame . . . Water alone gave him his horizon.[8]

But with Hoffmann it was different. His water fired and flamed. In fact his personal tale matches the saying of the Muse of Poetry in the opera by Offenbach, *Tales of Hoffmann*. The Muse says that, in concert with the spirits of beer and wine, "the human no longer exists, rather now one is a poet." Hoffmann, a true poet, died at age forty-six, a confirmed drunk. While alive, his grotesque poetries were drawn directly from the punch bowl, as a critic named Sucher has accurately noted.[9] Bachelard thus speaks of alcohol as a "triumph of the thaumaturgical activity of human thought." He writes:

> Brandy, or *eau de vie,* is also *eau de feu* or fire-water. It is a water which burns the tongue and flames up at the slightest spark. It does not limit itself to dissolving and destroying as does *aqua fortis.* It disappears with what it burns. It is the communion of life and of fire. Alcohol is also an immediate food which quickly warms the cockles of the heart: in comparison with alcohol, even meats are slow acting. . . . For the drinker of the *brûlot* how poor and cold and obscure is the experience of the drinker of hot tea! [10]

If the clue from poetry concerning drunkenness is in the phrase "fire water," then the work of moistening must have two sides to it. First, there is the fire to be found in the flowing, in the flux, in the moistenings of life. Second, there is also a moistening which happens when we are warm, warmed, and warming, a sort of liquification of self when things are sensed to be combustible. Baudelaire is a well-known witness to the first of these, as Hoffmann gives testimony to the second. A poetics of drunkenness includes both at once. In the following two chapters each will be explored separately.

25 THE FIRE IN WATER: RHYTHM'S IN-BETWEEN

BAUDELAIRE places the image of drunkenness precisely within the problem of "time." "One must always be drunk," he writes.

> That's all there is to it; that's the only solution. In order not to feel the horrible burden of Time breaking your shoulders and bowing your head to the ground, you must be drunken without respite.

Then the poet shows his teaching/preaching to be poetic by asking:

> But with what? With wine, poetry or virtue, as you will. Be you drunken.

To be sure, life will not always seem this way. That is, it will not always be sensed by us as being drunk. But Baudelaire speaks to this lack:

> If sometimes you awake, on the steps of a palace, in the green herbage of a ditch or in the dreary solitude of your room, then ask

the wind, the waves, the stars, the birds, the clocks, ask everything that runs, that moans, that moves on wheels, everything
that sings and speaks—ask them what is the time of day; and the
wind, the waves, the stars, the birds and the clocks will answer
you: "It is time to get drunk. In order not to be the martyred slave
of Time, be you drunken; be you drunken ceaselessly! With
wine, poetry or virtue, as you will.[1]

What is the function of this poetic drunkenness? How does it
fire the flow of life? How does it fill the time?

Arthur Rimbaud and Paul Verlaine give answer in their verse.
In a poem entitled, "The Drunken Boat," Rimbaud writes
about a "body drunk with moisture" (*la carcasse ivre d'eau*). He
speaks of a "tempest which blessed my journey over the water"
(*le tempête a béni mes éveils maritimes*). The poet notes that in
the soul's tempest a person "bathes in the poem of the sea" and
he thereby discovers a "blessing in this drunk, moist tempest of
life"—the blessing of "slow and delerious rhythms which are
stronger than alcohol and vaster than a lyre's music."[2]

So also Verlaine, in a work which became the so-called "bible" for the Symbolist Movement, writes: "In music, before
anything else ... Music yet and forever!" And the music for
which the poet wishes is one with a drunken rhythm. He says:
Préfère l'impair ("the uneven rhythm is best").[3]

Poetry is music, and its best meter is that which is uneven, or
drunken, like Rimbaud's boat. The case of a grace note in music
is an instance of this idea. Is a grace note in time or out of time,
in the rhythm or out? It is certainly part of the rhythm. In fact, it
shows the rhythm, highlights it, "graces" it, one might say. Yet it
is neither in nor out of the beat, the beating. It is the grace of the
beat. It notes the rhythm's grace apart from and yet not apart
from the beating. It is a filling of music's time, the music of time.
It notes the grace in time fulfilled, experienced in the rhythm of
every grace note, an intoxication of the music.

So the poetry says: if time is empty, be drunk, or, more precisely, look for the drunkenness which already exists. In drunk-

enness one senses the missing rhythm, water's fire in the flux itself. So Wallace Stevens can say of "music that is not yet written but is to be" (meaning by this the poems that he has as yet not been able to achieve) that it "needed the heavy nights of drenching weather." [4] And Rilke puts it this way: "Explore and win / Knowledge of transformation through and through. / What experience was the worst for you? Is thinking bitter, you must turn to wine." [5] There is fire in this poet's water. Poetry shows a rhythm in life. Or, as Rilke says: poetry is "the counterweight in which I happen to myself rhythmically." [6]

The rhythm of drunkenness is strange. It has to do with flow, to be sure, as the Greek word *rhythmos* (= "flow") already tells. But is it not our habit to think of rhythm as happening in percussion's beats? Whereas the poetic moistening of drunken rhythm is in-between, a flux between the moments of sobriety, a moistening of percussive moments. The drunken rhythm is a tempest (Rimbaud). It is uneven (Verlaine). Poetry leads us to see the rhythm between the beats, as if the ego's markings did not exist in life's truly staggering reality. In metaphor *all* is transistory. If Martin Heidegger can say that "poetry conceals a hidden essence which appears as rhythm," [7] perhaps we could also express the corollary: that rhythm is hidden between any essences that may appear to ego-consciousness.

In fact, musicologist Victor Zuckerkandl makes this very point concerning the music of rhythm. He writes:

> Our interest is not in the dividing points but in what goes on *between* them. We discover that it is not in the demarcating beats but where at first we did not look at all, where nothing happens, where *time simply passes*—it is in the apparent vacuum between the demarcating beats that musical meter is born. [8]

Zuckerkandl goes on in this argument by correcting the diction in his last sentence. He says that in fact he is not really speaking about *meter* at all. It is rather rhythm he is after. He even observes that a certain kind of *time* is suffocated by real musical rhythm of high quality. Meter disappears. He follows the idea of Ludwig Klages, from a work entitled *Vom Wesen des Rhythmus* ("On the Essence of Rhythm"), by saying: "A machine runs metrically; but man walks rhythmically." Zuckerkandl concludes: "Rhythm is an *experience* of time."[9]

Drunken rhythm—we might then suppose—is the experience of filled time. It may be seen as the "time" whose meter is not that of some mechanical clock or machine. Drunken rhythm, like the rhythm of good music, happens in some between, where nothing is being marked by ego's mode of consciousness, nothing, that is, except grace!

This fantasy of "betweenness," witnessed to by poet and musicologist, is curious. It has to do with the filling of time by an empty-between. Yet, however paradoxical the language which reports this experience may sound, it nonetheless is attempting to tell straightforwardly of a life-experience widely attested. Heraclitus speaks of god as being *between* sun and moon, winter and summer, war and peace, satiety and want.[10] The Hindu text *Brahmanah Parimarah* speaks of "holy power" as being in moments *between* lightning and rain, rain and moon, moon and sun, sun and hearth-fire.[11] In *The Republic*, Plato talks about a *metaxy*, "an intermediate realm," as being a place of soul (*psychē*). And in *The Symposium* he uses the same word to speak of the place one will find Love (*Eros*).[12] Pascal spoke of man's true existence as being *between* two infinites, the infinitely large and the infinitely small,[13] and Heidegger used the German words for "between" (*zwischen* and *zwischenfall*) to describe the situation in which an authentic poetic self finds itself.[14]

According to Heidegger, the *zwischen*-realm is experienced as a "rift" in life (*Riss*). But these rifts or cleavages are at the same time a sense of "openness" and a "clearing" in life's "dark woods" (*Lichtung, Unterwegs*). Such experiences happen to us as conflict and wrestling, and yet it is not a "mere cleft being ripped open."

> Rather, it is the intimacy with which opponents belong to each other. This rift carries the opponents into the course of their unity by virtue of their common ground.[15]

The "rift," then, is the experience of "nothing" (*Nichts*). But it is a "nothingness" which we scarcely know.[16] It is an "emptiness" which is essential to our being.[17] The empty nothing of life's meaning is the "region" in which meaning is in fact "gathered" and "bears itself to encounter emptiness in such a way that in and through that experience mountains appear."[18] It is a "wide sphere" of life in which we achieve a "rhythm" or a "swing" (*Schwingungsbereich*). The "swing" or rhythm of life is felt as "mortals go to and fro slowly."[19] Slowness gives a "ring" or resonance to life-experience. It is the dance of meaning,[20] a dance which, according to Heidegger's imagery, is "time's removing" and "space's throwing open" in a "play of stillness," like Silenos' "calm drunkenness."[21]

So it may be imagined that *only* in the *nothingness* of the *between*-moments can a fullness of meaning come to be in life, for only there is the sounding-box of Being hollow enough to make the soundless music audible to stilled-ego, as in the case, for example, of the wondrously, pregnantly empty blue guitar of Picasso and Wallace Stevens.

Or, take the case of Heidegger's vessel, the image of a wine-jug. "We become aware of the vessel's holding-nature when we fill the jug," says Heidegger:

> The jug's bottom and sides obviously take on the task of holding. But not so fast! When we fill the jug with wine, do we pour the wine into the sides and bottom? . . . Sides and bottom are, to be sure, what is impermeable in the vessel. But what is impermeable is not yet what does the holding. When we fill the jug, the pouring that fills it flows into the empty jug. The emptiness, the void, is what does the vessel's holding. The empty space, this

nothing of the jug, is what the jug is as the holding vessel. . . .
Only a vessel . . . can empty itself. . . . The potter . . . shapes the
void.[22]

This way of seeing is a way of sensing real life-experience. It
suggests that "time" is "filled," not when we look to the various
some-wheres of life, but rather when we sense our being as if
between two wheres, or whens, or whos, or whats. The fullness
is sensed in the moment of apparent emptying which is not a
tabula rasa but rather a *plēroma*. When life seems to go empty
for us we may begin to feel the fullness which was there all
along. In such moments of "time" we sense a rhythm, not in our
customary beatings, but now in the moistening drunkenness of
sense. It all catches fire in the flow!

The music intoxicates, and the intoxication makes music's
rhythm. It happens in the moistening drunkenness. There is
fire already and always in that water, if we could only sense the
rhythm, a rhythm in the flow that deprives us of our ego-
concerns for meter (quantity) and measuring (judgment).[23]

26 THE WATER OF FIRE: AN ART OF FORGETTING

THE same poetry which knows the fire in the water knows something else about fire-water, too. It knows a moisturizing sense in the flamings of life whose heat may ordinarily seem to make life dry. Fire's water is sensed as an inundation, a dying which happens in the various warm experiences of living. It manifests itself, this water of the fire, this flood of heat, in an experience every drunk knows all too well: the experience of the loss of memory. A watery, dissolving forgetting accompanies intoxication's fire. The curious thing is that poets celebrate this forgetting in just the same way that Silenos teaches dying.

For example, in the opera *Tales of Hoffmann*, the poet himself says: "Ah! I am fire! . . . There comes to me a divine vertigo from the spirits of alcohol, from beer, and from wine! There comes a drunkenness in the folly of nothingness by which my soul is able to forget!"[1] This celebration of forgetting is like

Rilke's elegy in which a lover's kiss is likened to "drink upon drink: in which the drinker (i.e., the lover) goes out of himself ecstatically."[2] In a *Sonnet to Orpheus,* the same poet says that "only the dead drink" (reminiscent of the teaching of drunk Silenos), because in death, the poet goes on, "we are beckoned by the god to the flowing source of all things."[3]

It is as if a function of fire-water is a dying in which one senses the god, like a love-affair wherein psyche discovers itself deeply in some forgetting of ego. Just how this lethal forgetting is in fact experience as a pleromatic filling of soul's time is expressed by an odd tradition in Oriental poetry.[4]

Tao Yuan-Ming was a poet-hermit-farmer in late fourteenth-century China. He loved children, chrysanthemums, and wine. He possessed a grave manner, and like Pu Tai and many other fat and laughing Buddhas after him, he had a queer streak of humor and preferred autumn to other seasons. He spent eighty-three days as chief officer of his district, but then his sister died, and he went home.[5]

Yuan-Ming wrote a poem about P'eng Tsu who was great-grandson to the emperor, Chuan Hsu, who lived in the third millenium BCE. P'eng Tsu had ninety wives and was over eight hundred years old when he disappeared in the West. He had had a full time! About him, Yuan-Ming wrote: "Ceaseless drunkenness brings forgetfulness."[6] Perhaps it was just this full forgetfulness for which Yuan-Ming himself yearned when he said, in "Elegy for Myself," "all I regret is that I did not drink like a prodigal."[7]

The forgetfulness and the drinking are themselves pictured as a prodigality. For Yuan-Ming they are matters of soul, as is expressed in the song called "Drunk and Sober."

> *A guest resides in me,*
> *Our interests are not altogether the same.*
> *One of us is always drunk:*
> *The other is always awake.*
> *Awake and drunk—*
> *We laugh at one another,*
> *And we do not understand each other's world.*[8]

Here the forgetfulness of drinking connects with self's forgetting of ego. It is a dying, to be sure, a moistening of the fire.

Two poems by Yuan-Ming make this clear. The first is called, "Chrysanthemums"; the second, "The Return."

> *The wine is poured when the cup is empty.*
> *And everyone is silent at the setting of the sun.*[9]

Forgetting is the silencing of solar ego, the setting of the sun in an emptying cup. For Yuan-Ming this is cause to celebrate, as the second poem notes:

> *I empty the cup and lean on the window*
> *And joyfully contemplate my favorite branches.*[10]

The emptied cup (drunkenness of self in the face of sobered ego) enables the joy which comes from seeing the branches in flower!

Even if this could be experienced, it is not an easy thing to understand a forgetting which fills soul with feelings, thought, image, fantasies, and warmth. It is not easy because how could it be that one could experience time's fullness, a chrysanthemum of flowering soul, in forgetting, in the empty cup of drunkenness' dying? This question presents itself because Western fantasies concerning "time" have taught us that forgetting is opposite to remembering.[11]

This oppositional fantasy puts the experience of forgetting in an inferior position, making it seem ineluctably a negative matter. But the forgetting which comes in poetic drunkenness, as in the case of Yuan-Ming, the emptiness which makes possible the seeing of a flower-bud blooming on a branch, is a special thing in itself. It is not the negative side of a memory which is judged to be positive. The poetics of drunkenness suggests a different fantasy concerning forgetting, something perhaps more akin to the ideal of "The Great Forgetting" about which Asian religious texts speak.

Perhaps our Western language can reconnect us to this other fantasy, one which releases the experience of forgetting from the memory-versus-forgetting complex where it is judged to be merely negative. Both Greek and English terminology indicate a people's experience of forgetting which has little to do with memory, not even being its opposite. To be sure, there is in Greek the word *lesmosyne,* which is opposite to *mnemosyne,* and *amnesis* which is opposed to *anamnesis.* There is indeed a memory-forgetting idea in life. But there is also something altogether different. It is indicated by the words, *Lēthē* and *lanthanomai,* which also mean "forgetting," but which have no opposites in language or idea.

Lēthē is associated, not to memory, being its opposite, but rather to truth (*a-lētheia*), as if there were a forgetting which is intimately linked to the experience of truth. *Lēthē* is the river which leads to the underworld. It is the water or moisture by which one discovers a journey to the deep world of soul. It takes the self across to a place of deep hiddenness (*lanthanosai*), to the under-world of Hades, the place where truth (*a-lētheia*) is unveiled (*a-lanthanomai*). It is in this experience that there is something deep and hidden to ego's everyday life of consciousness. Something is secreted and guarded and preserved in this soul-realm.[12]

The point is that in this Lethean fantasy of the Greek language, forgetting is dislodged from the complex of ideas and feelings that we have about memory. These two are no longer seen in relation to each other at all. Forgetting, therefore, is hardly to be overcome or cured by memory. Rather, the fateful lethal moistening is precisely that which gives soul to life.

That such a gain in soul is also a gain in a sense of body is implied by the English language. The word "forget" is not *linguistically* opposite to the word "remember." The opposite of "remember" in language's fantasy is "dismember." Our word "forget" refers to something in itself, something in fact closer to the original meaning of the word "remember" than we might suppose as long as we are gripped by the idea that these are opposites. "Forget" is in Old English "for-gitan," which in turn is taken from a long line of ancestor-words: *vergessen,* in German; *gataim,* in Old Iranian; *praehendere,* in Latin; *khanda-*

nein, in Greek; etc. All these stem from the Indo-European root, *ghed-,* meaning "to hold," "to grasp," "to take," "to steal," or "to seize."[13]

The fantasy governing this linguistic family is that there is a grasping, seizing, and taking going on in life. But sometimes the "for-" prefix, meaning "omission," may be sensed in relation to this ego-manner of being. "Forgetting" then would express the experience of letting-go, a for-getting of the getting, the grasping, and the seizing. In short, "for-getting" names the times when ego-perspective dies.

Yuan-Ming's saying that his only regret was that he did not drink like a prodigal is tantamount to saying that he regretted that there were not more forgettings, more moments in which his sense of self was ruled by a perspective other than that of ego, a time deepened by Lethe's soul and humbled by forgetting's letting go. Perhaps it is in *this* forgetting that chrysanthemums appear. Life flowers! Such a forgetting would be, not opposite to memory, but precisely itself a re-membering. Not only is it a sensing of soul, but it also puts body back into things, membering that which was obscured by ego's ideas and feelings, its opinions and fancies.

The point might be that the poetic fantasy of drunkenness leads to a sense of forgetting released from opposition to the notion of having to remember. In fact, it may lead to a seeing of forgetting *as* remembering. Drunkenness, in this view, becomes the image of the art of forgetfulness: an *ars memoria.*

The art of forgetfulness of ego is the silenic rhythm of firewater. Silenos' teaching about the importance of dying as soon as possible after ego is born in us becomes clear. It says that unless we die to ego's perspectives, we may miss the chrysanthemum's amazement. The great teacher, Silenos, in the cave of self, seems to know that in the fullness of time there is no fire apart from water and no moisture without flaming. We may have to die to learn his teaching . . . or be drunk . . . or rather, embrace the dying and the drunkenness that is already experienced in the cave of psyche.

27 THE ARROW OF INTOXICATION AND THE NICK OF TIME

THIS matter began many chapters ago as a quest for an image of the Great Teacher who teaches the fullness of time. It led to a discovery, or perhaps an admission of certain times in which time seems empty, a situation felt to be contrary to the nature of the Great Teacher's teaching. In such times, preaching is split off from teaching, the two being viewed as separate activities. The search for an image which would bring these two into relation with each other brought us to the cave of Silenos, an archetypal and mythical figure of the Teacher. But it led to drunkenness, too, a silenic shadow.

Then drunkenness was itself probed as an image. It was sensed to depict a moistening flowing, a flux, a non-literal reality in which all things are intoxicated. There were two sides to this image of drunkenness: a fire in life's moistures, and a moistening in warmth.

But, finally, what has this silenic fire-water to do with preaching and teaching? with images of the Great Teacher? and with the fullness of time?

Perhaps the poetry which carries silenic wisdom into our time can give us a new way of viewing preaching and teaching. Ordinarily preaching is seen as a matter of "fire," a fiery matter, whether the preaching is a work of ecclesiastical or of political rhetoric, or even of the work of the "preacher" within each person. It is the out-loud, standing-up, publicizing expression of a burning matter. Fire and brimstone! Something comes out in the open in preaching.

Teaching, on the other hand, is customarily sensed as moisture's way, giving "solutions," as one says, "dissolving" problems, making it flow with logic or with explanation. So it is with "pro-fessors" in all walks of life, and with those "teachers" within, whose explanations put out the fire so often, attempting, as they do, to "solve." It may therefore be, in the usual view, that the fire of the preacher within or without *dis*connects from the water of the teacher of self or society.

But the view of the Great Teacher which has been developing in the meditation of this work is altogether different from these usual notions, ideas we unwittingly inherit. Since Silenos' fire is found precisely in solutions and since his moist flowing is exactly located in flame, his preaching is teaching and his teaching is a proclamation or testimony.

Could it be that when we sense a teaching lacking in our preachings, not learning anything from them, that we might begin to look for the dying flux in our own fiery-ness? Or, could it be that when we begin to sense preaching's testimony and witness lacking in our education, we might now look for the warmth in our various solutions? Perhaps we could begin to sense some rhythm in life, not in the percussive beatings of preachment, but in between the flames which fire us. Or, maybe we could begin to sense education, not as everything to be remembered, but in the experience of forgetting, where we really learn. Then the preaching within might become rhythm for teaching, just in the moistened moments of every between, and the teaching within might become an art of forgetting the inner preacher's over-heated fire. It may all be something like fire-water's intoxication, a Silenos speaking out of the needs in the cave of self and world: a recovery of an image of a Great Teacher in whom an inner teacher and preacher, though forever at war, each want and need the other.

Thus it would be that a poetics of fire-water remythologizes Christ silenically. It is not only a matter of noting, with Luke, that the Son of Man came, like Lot and Noah, eating and drinking.[1] Nor is it only a question of seeing the intimate relation between calling Christ a Great Teacher (*didaskalos agathe*) and his referring to himself as the True Vine (*ampelos alethine*).[2] Even more, Silenos' rhythms in the world of christic imagination are caught in the words which are not unlike those that Midas heard from the Greek god: "Whoever seeks to gain his life will lose it, but whoever loses his life will preserve it."[3]

Yet a question still remains. How are the rhythms of forgetting, of losing ego's life-perspectives, of the drunkenness that sobers self to be experienced as filling time with soul and body? A clue to this is secreted in the word *kairos* itself, the word with which we began this part of the book and with which we now end.

Mark's Gospel uses the word *kairos* to mean "filled time." It is indeed the case that this term came to mean "due measure," "fitness," "opportunity," and so on. But it is used earlier by Aeschylus, for example, in a context where it can only be adequately translated as "target," or "mark," since in the dramatist's sentence it is the object of an arrow shot from a bow.[4] In fact, Euripides says at one place that man is as *eis kairon tupeis*, "struck in his target."[5] So the Roman peoples translated *kairos* by their word, *tempus*, which is not only a word for "time," but also gives us the term, "temple." *Tempus* is the place where penetration is easiest, to the divine or to the body. Homer, for example, used *kairos* to indicate the place in man's body where a weapon could penetrate deepest for the vulnerability of life within ("temple" in the head).[6] We might call it an "opening" or a "loophole."

So, also, *kairos* (with a different vocal accent in Greek) meant the momentary *opening* in the warp-threads of a loom through which the woof-spindle was shot like an arrow by the expert weaver. This moment is the fateful moment, the weaving of fate and destiny. It happens at just the right time and takes a proper rhythm, hitting *between* the threads.

Pindar used the word, *kairos*, to mean an opening in anything, as English, too, uses the term, "nick" or "chink," as in a "chink in armor," or, "in the nick of time." Odysseus, in the shooting contest for the hand of Penelope, aimed at the kairotic nick, the aperture in twelve axes, just as Jael slew Sisera by driving a tent-peg through the weakest point in his skull, that is, in his temple.[7] The target is a hole, an opening, a "between." Or, one might imagine, the crucial time in life is the rhythm of emptiness when man is struck by some intoxication which is an arrow of a Great Teacher, the arrow of God.

The English word, "intoxicate," carries the point of such an experience of "time" (*kairos*). "Intoxicate" means, of course, to be "in" a "poison" (*toxic*). But the original Greek term, *toxikon*, refers to a very special substance, a particular poison. It is that which is put on the tip of an arrow. The Greek word is formed from *toxikos*, which in the beginning did not have poisonous or moralistic connotations at all. It meant simply, "of the bow." The *toxon* was the bow and arrow itself. It was the arrow shot by the bow into the *kairos*, into the opening target, into the emptiness. It was fate's arrow, a shaft of intoxication shot by some god in the nick of time.

Indeed, it is like the bow which appears in the moist rain that God sent to Noah. It is a fire in the flood: the fire of the sun and the water of the moon come together in the fire-water of the rainbow! It happens in the nick of time: a rain-bow's arrow hitting the kairotic mark, a drunkening of reality. The moistening fire and a warming, flaming moisture!

One might paraphrase Shakespeare on this fantasy. To drink

or not to drink is *not* the question: rather, 'tis nobler in soul to suffer the slings and arrows of outrageous fortune, and to lay down arms against the troubling waters of life's intoxications which never end in time.

The fullness of time is an emptiness! Empty moments in life may disclose to us a fullness.[8] Such is one way time is fulfilled (*kairos peplērotai*). It all goes drunk in rhythms of ego's forgetting.

Time, then, is itself a Great Teacher: a silenic christos! It is herald and didact in one, both preacher and teacher experienced within.[9] This teacher in time gets us in our temples, penetrating the body of soul. We die to remember this forgetting, to learn this lesson of letting go, that precisely when there is nothing more to preach, nothing more to teach, an arrow of outrageous fortune strikes the chink of ego's armor.[10] It is a full cup, this emptying, toxic to the grasping literalisms of ego's perspective.

Its Great Teacher is a vine. When he bleeds, it is wine . . . or perhaps a chrysanthemum.

NOTES

Introduction: The Idea of a Polytheistic, Archetypal Theology

1. Wallace Stevens, "July Mountain," *Opus Posthumous* (New York: Alfred A. Knopf, 1977), pp. 114f.

2. Wallace Stevens, "The Owl and the Sarcophagus," II, *The Collected Poems* (New York: Alfred A. Knopf, 1975), pp. 432ff.

3. From: "Of Ideal Time and Choice," written in the same year as "The Owl and the Sarcophagus" (1947). This poem is neither in *The Collected Poems* nor in the *Opus Posthumous*. But it appears in: *Palm at the End of the Mind,* ed. Holly Stevens (New York: Vintage Books, 1972), p. 300.

4. David L. Miller, *The New Polytheism* (New York: Harper and Row, Publishers, 1974). A second edition is forthcoming from Spring Publications (Dallas, Texas), and there is a French edition in print: *Le nouveau polythéisme* (Paris: Éditions Imago, 1979).

5. Aristotle, *Metaphysics*, Lambda 8.1074^{a}38–^{b}14; Beta 4.1000^{b}9–19. For other sources of this axiom, see: Werner Jaeger, *The Theology of the Early Greek Philosophers* (New York: Oxford University Press, 1967), and *Early Christianity and Greek Paideia* (New York: Oxford University Press, 1969). Also: Miller, *The New Polytheism*, Chapter III.

6. T. S. Eliot, *The Complete Poems and Plays: 1909–1950* (New York: Harcourt, Brace and Co., 1952), p. 133.

7. C. G. Jung, *Collected Works* (hereafter, *CW*), XI.148 (referring to volume and paragraph number).

8. *The Freud-Jung Letters,* ed. W. McGuire (Princeton: Princeton University Press, 1974), p. 294. Compare Jung's letter of January 13, 1948: "I thank God every day that I have been permitted to experience the reality of the *imago Dei* in me. Had that not been so, I would be a bitter enemy of Christianity and of the Church in particular. Thanks to this *actus gratiae* my life has meaning, and my inner eye was opened to the beauty and grandeur of dogma." Cited in: *C. G. Jung: Word and Image,* ed. A. Jaffé (Princeton: Princeton University Press, 1979), p. 209.

9. This strategy of restoring a sense of meaning to ideas is by no means new. In the ancient world Proclus had spoken of the task of *epistrophē*, whereby a "reversion" of the "elements" of theology will bring them by "likeness" near to their source. In our own time the philosopher, Martin Heidegger, has engaged in a program of a recovery of the "remembering" of Being which has been forgotten. Ortega y Gassett, the Spanish philosopher, likens this strategy to that of the bullfighter who gains perspective at the critical moment of confrontation of the animal by "stepping back" before the kill. Freud found it a therapy, a making conscious of what is unconscious, to lead an individual case-history back to mythic likeness in Oedipus. Jung, too, viewed his patients as being grounded archetypally in mythic motifs of the collective unconscious. James Hillman speaks of the task of "archetypal psychology" as that of "reversion." In teaching the History of Religions, Henry Corbin follows the path of the Sufi master, Ibn Arabi, in the work of *ta'-wil,* which Corbin translates by the French words *ramener* and *reconduire,* that is, "leading back."

10. Those who know the work of Stanley Romaine Hopper will recognize in what follows a resemblance to his expression of a three-part movement: the steps *back* and *down* and *through.* See: "Le cri de Merlin!" in: J. Strelka, ed., *Yearbook of Comparative Literature,* Volume IV (University Park: Pennsylvania State University Press, 1971), pp. 9–35.

11. Origen, *Peri archōn* ("On First Principles"), III.vi.1; compare also: Origen, *Contra Celsum,* IV.30; Irenaeus, *Adv. haer.,* V.6; and, Clement of Alexandria, *Stromata,* II.38.5. On seeing the "likeness" of "images," see additionally: Hillman, "An Inquiry into Image," *Spring 1977* (Dallas), 62–88; and, "Further Notes on Images," *Spring 1978* (Dallas), 152–182.

12. The line is from Rainer Maria Rilke, and in the original reads: *erweckten sie uns . . . ein Gleichnis.* See: *Duino Elegies,* IX.105. Compare Stevens' lines given earlier in the Introduction: "If of substance, a likeness of the earth, / That by resemblance twanged him through and through." Also, recall the final lines of Goethe's *Faust: Alles vergängliches / Ist nur ein Gleichnis* ("Everything that passes before you is just a likeness").

13. See: Amos Niven Wilder, *Theopoetic* (Philadelphia: Fortress Press, 1976), where the author says: "I believe I had picked up the terms 'theopoetic' and 'theopoesis' from Stanley Hopper and his students, no doubt in one or another of the remarkable consultations of hermeneutics and language which he had organized at Drew and Syracuse to which so many of us are indebted."

14. It would be an unforgivable omission not to mention that what is here imagined as an archetypal, polytheistic theopoetic was begun brilliantly by a group of European Roman Catholic theologians at the start of this century. Hugo Rahner's name is perhaps best known of this group in America. His work, and that of his circle, are very important to the present project. See: Hugo Rahner, S.J., *Greek Myths and Christian Mystery* (New York: Harper and Row, 1963); R. Reitzenstein, *Die hellenistischen Mysterien nach ihren Grundgedanken und Wirkungen* (Leipzig, 1910); *Die Vorgeschichte der christlichen Taufe* (Leipzig, 1929); K. Prümm, *Der christliche Glaube und die altheidnische Welt* (Leipzig, 1935), *Das Christentum als Neuheitserlebnis: Durchblick durch die christlich-antike Begegnung* (Freiburg, 1939), *Das antike Heidentum nach seinen Grundströmungen* (Munich, 1942); and, generally, the issues of *Zeitschrift für katholische Theologie* in the thirties and forties.

15. Miller, *The New Polytheism,* pp. 71f.

16. See: Marcus Aurelius, *Meditations,* VII.2, where he urges one to discover religious doctrines in *fantasies* of the soul, for it is here that God lives!

17. Henry Corbin, "Pour une charte de l'imaginal," *Corps spirituel et terre céleste,* deuxième édition (Paris: Éditions Buchet/Chastel, 1979), pp. 7–19.

18. Stevens, *Opus Posthumous,* pp. 66f.

19. Ibid., p. 69.

1 Perfectionism and the Imitatio Christi

1. Mark 10:18; Luke 18:19 (all Biblical citations will be from the Revised Standard Version unless otherwise indicated). The parallel passage in Matthew 19:17 is only slightly different: "One there is who is good." Concerning this Biblical double-bind, Martin Foss writes: "This extreme, this most irrational demand [to love even one's enemies] is characterized by the frigid symbol of intellectual balance and order [i.e., perfection]." See: *The Idea of Perfection in the Western World* (Princeton: Princeton University Press, 1946), p. 29.

2. Alan Watts, *Beyond Theology* (New York: Pantheon, 1964). pp. 83–107, and *Psychotherapy East and West* (New York: Mentor, 1963), Chapter V.

3. See: Lala K. K. Dey, *The Intermediary World and Patterns of Perfection in Philo and Hebrews* (SBL Dissertation Series #25; Missoula: Scholars Press, 1975), p. 133 and *passim.*

4. See: John Passmore, *The Perfectibility of Man* (New York: Scribners, 1970), pp. 20f.

5. *Stromata*, VII.14; compare, Irenaeus, *Adv. haer.*, V.vi.1; and, *The Didachē*, I, VI, X, and XVI.

6. Passmore, *op. cit.*, pp. 68f.

7. On this history, in addition to the work of Passmore that has already been cited, see: Martin Foss, *op. cit.*; R. N. Flew, *The Idea of Perfection in Christian Theology* (New York: Humanities Press, 1968); J. L. Peters, *Christian Perfection and American Methodism* (Nashville: Abingdon, 1956).

8. Cited in: *The Hastings Encyclopedia* (New York: Scribners, 1917), Volume IX, p. 730.

9. Paul Tillich, *Systematic Theology* (Chicago: University of Chicago Press, 1963), Volume III, p. 241.

10. Passmore, *op. cit.*, Chap. XV and *passim.*

11. America is especially the manifestation of perfectionism following the Christian Protestant revivalism of the 1840's. John Wesley had spoken of a perfectionist climate which he hoped might "pervade the newly planted societies in America." See: Peters, *op. cit.*, pp. 188ff.

12. See the discussion of this textual issue in: Flew, *op. cit.*, pp. 4f.

2 The Good Shepherd and His Sheep

1. For example, see: *The Shepherd of Hermas*, Mandate II.6; XII.iii.3; Similitude II.7; V.ii.6; and especially, Vision II.ii.5.

2. Compare Euripides, *Ion*, 227f, where in order to attain access to the inner, sacred shrine at Delphi one must sacrifice a sheep.

3. See: Pierre de Bourget, S.J., *Early Christian Painting* (New York: Viking/Compass, 1965), p. 12 and figs. 15, 24, 27, 39, and *passim.*

Compare the material assembled in: Rudolf Bultmann, *The Gospel of John: A Commentary*, trans. Beaseley-Murry (Oxford: Blackwell, 1971), p. 370, ftn. 3.

4. Gerald Vann, O.P., *The Paradise Tree* (New York: Sheed and Ward, 1959), p. 179.

5. Cited in: Gerhard Friedrich, ed., *Theological Dictionary of the New Testament*, trans. G. Bromiley (Grand Rapids: Eerdmans, 1968), Volume VI, p. 486.

6. *Iliad*, II.243; compare Pindar's *Eighth Nemean Ode*, 6, where Aphrodite is referred to as *poimenes*, "shepherdess."

7. *Republic* 343a, b; compare sections 345c, d.

8. For example: Jeremiah 2:8; 3:15; compare Genesis 49:24; 48:15; and, Psalm 80.1.

9. See: John Barrell and John Bull, eds., *A Book of English Pastoral Verse* (New York: Oxford University Press, 1975), *passim*.

10. These lines are from the work of Breton, cited in: Richard Aldington, ed., *The Viking Book of Poetry* (New York: Viking, 1959), Volume I, p. 89.

11. C. G. Jung, *Collected Works* (hereafter, *CW*), XI.715 (referring to volume and paragraph numbers).

12. Cited in: Friedrich, ed., *op. cit.*, p. 489, ftn. 42.

13. Cited in: ibid., ftn. 41.

14. Ibid., pp. 488f.

15. Zechariah 10:3; 11:9; 13:7.

16. *The Interpreter's Bible* (Nashville: Abingdon, 1066), Volume VI, p. 1102. The interpreter is Robert Dentan.

17. Bultmann, *op. cit.*, pp. 312, 358–380.

18. These Mandean materials are cited in: ibid., pp. 368f.

19. Molière, *Le Bourgeois gentilhomme*, in: Charles H. Wall, ed., *The Dramatic Works of Molière* (London: Bell, 1911) Volume III, p. 163.

20. *As You Like It*, II.iv.61.

3   The Shepherd's Single Eye and Imitations

1. See: Barrell-Bull, eds., *op. cit.*, pp. 132f.

2. Walther Völker, *Fortschrift und Vollendung bei Philo von Alexandrien* (Leipzig: Hinrich, 1938), p. 263. Compare: Dey, *op. cit.*, p. 45, ftn. 4.

3. Passmore, *op. cit.*, p. 28.

4. Cited in: Dey, *op. cit.*, p. 133, compare pp. 129ff.

5. Cited in: ibid., p. 132. In the opinion of the French scholar, Epicq, this view of Philo's corresponds exactly with that of the New Testament. Epicq says: "The revelation of God made to ancient men and the revelation made by God through His Son are opposed to each other in the same way that imperfection and transitoriness are opposed to perfection and to that which is definite" (see: ibid., p. 129, ftn. 1).

6. *The Shepherd of Hermas,* Mandate IX.6.

7. Cited in: *Hastings Encyclopedia,* p. 729. A similar view is implied in the Aberkios Inscription from the third century. This funerary text reads: "I am called Aberkios. I am a pupil of the pure shepherd who feeds flocks of sheep on mountains and plains, who has great eyes, seeing in all places." (Cited in: Friedrich, ed., *op. cit.,* p. 497.)

8. Matthew 6:22. Compare: Passmore, *op. cit.,* pp. 142ff.

9. Cited in: Passmore, *op. cit.,* p. 143, ftn.

10. On the eye as a solar image, it being the "sun door penetration to the other world," and its relation to a sense of perfection imagined as "hitting the bull's eye," or "being on target," see: Joseph Campbell. *Masks of God: Occidental Mythology* (New York: Viking, 1964), p. 167. There is a connection here to the notion of sin, *hamartia,* as "missing the mark," an idea of imperfection that is dependent antecedently upon a sense of perfectionist obligation, which implies that it is a perfectionist view of imperfection.

11. Cited in: Passmore, *op. cit.,* p. 21.

12. See: Eric Partridge, ed., *Dictionary of Slang and Unconventional English* (New York: Macmillan, 1961), pp. 753f, 1267.

13. See: *The Compact Edition of the Oxford English Dictionary* (New York: Oxford Press, 1971), Volume II, pp. 2778f.

14. Cited in: ibid., p. 2783.

4 The End of Perfection

1. Compare the author's essay, "Images of Happy Ending," in: *Eranos 1975* (Volume XLIV; Leiden: E. J. Brill, 1977), pp. 61–89. Also see: G. W. H. Lampe, ed., *Patristic Greek Lexicon* (Oxford: Clarendon Press, 1968), Fasc. V, *teleios;* and compare: ibid., Fasc. I, *ateleia* and *atelē,* these being the words in Greek for "imperfection" and "not ended." For specific classical instances of usage, see: *Iliad,* I.66; Aristotle, *Metaphysics,* IV.16; Plato, *Cratylus,* 403e; Aeschylus, *The Suppliants,* 525f; Herodotus, I.183.2; Plato, *The Laws,* II.653a; and Aristotle, *The Ethics,* III. Martin Foss comments on connecting the ideas of "end" and "perfection" as being normative in the West. He cites Aristotle's *Metaphysics,* 1021b, and Aquinas' *De nom.,* I.3 ("Perfectio consistit in hoc quod pertingat ad finem"). See: Foss, *op. cit.,* p. 8.

2. *Theogony,* 637f. Compare: R. B. Onians, *The Origins of European Thought* (New York: Arno, 1973), pp. 426ff.

3. Onians, *op. cit.,* p. 440 and *passim.*

4. Compare the ideas of James Hillman who has spoken of "the end of analysis," a "utopian *telos* that can never be realized, because this process (ego development) has no end term unless it abandons the past analytical method. . . . All this means that analysis as we have known it is interminable." Hillman calls for a different perspective which he, not unlike later chapters of this work, suggests "means Tiresias and the sacrifice of the mind's bright eye so that we can see the images in the cavern of *memoria.*" See: Hillman, *Myth of Analysis* (Evanston: Northwestern University Press, 1972), pp. 291, 295.

5. Heraclitus, *Fragments,* #45 (Diels-Kranz' numbering).

5 Jesus the Model of Imperfection

1. Franz Kafka, *The Great Wall of China,* trans. Muir and Muir (New York: Schocken Books, 1970), p. 167.

2. Foss, *op. cit.,* pp. 60f. The relevant paragraphs in Kant's third *Critique* are #15, #16, and #23.

3. Jung, *CW,* IX.ii.68–126 (especially note Jung's treatment of the double-binding nature of the commandment in Matthew at paragraph #123 and #113). Compare the notion of *defectu* in the writings of St. Augustine, as observed by Stanley R. Hopper, in: R. Battenhouse, ed., *A Companion to the Study of St. Augustine* (New York: Oxford, 1955), pp. 162–164.

4. Compare the author's earlier work: *Gods and Games: Toward a Theology of Play* (New York: Harper and Row, 1973).

5. Jung, *CW,* XII.74, compare ftn. 4 above.

6. See the author's work, *The New Polytheism* (New York: Harper and Row, 1974), especially chapters I and II, and the Introduction to this book.

7. A phrase by Heraclitus implies a similar work with a two-sided complex. He said: "Dionysos and Hades are one." With this there is implied taking Hades out of the complex with his brother, Zeus, and taking Dionysos out of the complex with his brother, Apollo. The resulting new configuration releases a sense of that which is Dionysian from Apollonian rationalism (the former being thought of as the

negative of the latter) and it frees a sense of that which belongs deeply in Hades' underworld from the overarching "sky"-perspective of a transcendental, Olympian theology of Zeus (again, the former being viewed merely as the negative of the latter). Heraclitus is seeing here, in the fact that the Dionysian and the Underworldly belong to each other, what he elsewhere called a "hidden harmony." See: David L. Miller, "Hades and Dionysos: The Poetry of Soul," in: *Journal of the American Academy of Religion*, XLVI/3, 331–335.

8. Jung once argued for the image of Christ as a sense of imperfection rather than of perfection. He said: "We all must do just what Christ did. We must make our experiment. We must make mistakes. . . . And there will be error. If you avoid error you do not live; in a sense even it may be said that every life is a mistake, for no one has found the truth. When we live like this we know Christ as a brother, and God indeed becomes man. This sounds like a terrible blasphemy, but not so . . . for then only does God become man in ourselves." See: "Is Analytical Psychology a Religion?" *Spring 1972* (Dallas), p. 147.

6 Christ the Lamb and Hermes the Ram

1. See: Jung, *CW*, IX.ii, chapter VIII. Jung, in 1951, anticipated the present essay, announcing the thesis that will be developed in this chapter, but without arguing it. Jung claimed that Reitzenstein had already demonstrated the connection. See: R. Reitzenstein, *Poimandres: Studien zur Griechisch-Agyptischen und Früchristlichen Literatur* (Leipzig: Teubner, 1904). But in fact Reitzenstein limits his exploration of the shepherd-motif to the *Corpus hermeticum* and the texts parallel to it, never drawing the theological and psychological implications which are attempted here. See also: Jung, *CW* IX.ii. fig. #17, which pictures Hermes *artifex* as a Shepherd of Taurus and Aries. This picture is taken from: Thomas Aquinas (pseud.), *De alchimia*, a sixteenth-century manuscript, Codex Vossianus, XXIX (Leiden: University Bibliotek), folio 94a.

2. Now published in English as: Hugo Rahner, S.J., *Greek Myths and Christian Mystery* (New York: Harper and Row, 1963), Part II, especially pp. 181–222.

3. Justin, *Apology*, I.22; Hippolytus, *Elenchos*, IV.48.2; Pseudo-Clement, *Recognitiones*, X.41.

4. Rahner, *op. cit.*, p. 132, ftn. 3. See: Hippolytus, *Commentary on Daniel*, IV.23.

5. See pages 9–11 and 13, above, and, Rahner, *op. cit.*, p. 190, ftn. 3. Also: Karl Kerényi, *Hermes: Guide of Souls,* trans. Stein (Dallas: Spring Publications, 1976), pp. 82ff. The association of Hermes to the sheep is also demonstrated at length, in: E. R. Goodenough, *Jewish Symbols in the Greco-Roman Period: Volume VIII, Pagan Symbols in Judaism* (New York: Pantheon, 1958), pp. 71ff. For example, in the Viena Randanini catacomb in Rome, we see Hermes with his caduceus and a sheep and a bottle.

6. Pausanius, IX.22.1.

7. See: Pausanius, *Guide to Greece,* trans. P. Levi, S.J. (Baltimore: Penguin, 1971), Volume I, p. 353, fig. #22.

8. In fact there are whole series of gem-pictures which show Hermes as a ram. See: Kerényi, *op. cit.*, p. 86.

9. Pausanius, II.3.4.

10. Clement of Alexandria, *Protrepticus,* II.13.

11. E. R. Goodenough, *op. cit.*, Volume XII (1965), p. 146. For other discussion of the sexual quality of Hermes, see: Daniel C. Noel, "Veiled Kabir: C. G. Jung's Phallic Self-Image," in: *Spring 1974* (Dallas), 224ff.

12. Cited from: A study of sheep-motifs by a French scholar, A. Deiber, reported in: Goodenough, *op. cit.*, Vol. XII, p. 73.

13. Ibid., pp. 74–82.

14. Clement of Alexandria, *Paidagogos,* I.292; compare Goodenough, *op. cit.*, Vol. XII, p. 79; and, Rahner, *loc cit.*

15. See: Friedrich, ed., *op. cit.*, p. 490.

16. Apollodorus, I.80ff.

17. Hermes' activity here is like that of Artemis, who interceded at the moment of Iphigeneia's sacrifice by her father, Agamemnon. In this case it was a deer rather than a ram which was involved. See: Euripides, *Iphigeneia at Tauris.*

18. See: Robert Graves, *Greek Myths* (Baltimore: Penguin. 1955), section 70.

19. See: Genesis 22:1–14.

20. One may think in this regard of Apuleius' tale of Eros and Psyche, how Psyche's "death" was preceded by an encounter with the Rams of the Golden Fleece who, like the Hermes of Samothrace, initiate one into the bodily mystery of sexuality and who may be approached only when the sun is on the wane or in the darkness of night.

21. Jung, *CW,* XI.743.

22. Tillich, *op. cit.*, p. 241.

7 Christ the Shepherd and the Monster Cyclops

1. See: Emma Jung and M.-L. von Franz, *The Grail Legend*, trans. A. Dykes (New York: Putnam, 1970), p. 348.

2. See pages 15–18, above.

3. *Shepherd of Hermas*, Mandate IX.6.

4. Jung notes the association of shepherd and beastly monster, demonstrating parallels between the Shepherd of Hermas and Michael Maier's alchemical vision of this image. See: *CW*, XIV.301f.

5. Gösta Liebert, *Iconographic Dictionary of Indian Religions* (Leiden: Brill, 1976), pp. 302f. *Trinetra* and *Trilocana*, both meaning "three-eyed," are epithets of Shiva who is *trinayana* ("three-eyed"), the eyes representing sun, moon, and—the one in the center of the forehead—*agni* ("fire").

6. *Odyssey*, IX.106–365. For further discussion of the Greek mythological connection between the shepherd and the demonically grotesque, see: W. H. Roscher and James Hillman, *Pan and the Nightmare* (Dallas: Spring Publications, 1972), pp. 61–63, and *passim*.

7. *Odyssey*, IX.388–391. The translation here is that of Robert Fitzgerald: *The Odyssey* (Garden City: Doubleday, 1963), p. 156.

8. Ibid., p. 160.

9. Jung comments on this motif: "Osiris, the god of the underworld, also lost one eye. Wotan had to sacrifice one eye to the well of Mimir, the well of wisdom, which is the unconscious. You see one eye will remain in the depths or turned toward it. Therefore, Jakob Boehme, when he was 'enchanted into the center of nature,' as he said, wrote his book about the 'Reversed Eye.' One of his eyes was turned inward, and kept on looking into the underworld, which amounts to the loss of one eye; he no longer had two eyes for this world." See: "Commentary on Kundalini Yoga," in: *Spring 1976* (Dallas), 18f.

10. Norman O. Brown has brilliantly examined this complex from a different side, meditating the question: *Cur aliquid vidi?* ("Why did I have to see?") His approach is by way of the archetypal image of Actaeon. The link to this work is in the observations concerning the German phrase, *Augenspross am Hirschgeweih*, meaning "antlers" or "horns," but literally imaging "eye sprouts," according to the word's etymology. When the eye of the Cyclops is put out by Odysseus, the monster is left with an "eye sprout," which depicts a sort of inverted horn, a corona (the terms "horn" and "corn" being philologically the same). The voided head of Polyphemos is a cornucopia, the nothingness being a horn of plenty (see pages 138–58 below). There is a

symbolic association here to the horn of Hermes' ram and the horn of the Lamb in the Apocalypse of St. John and in the prophecy of Daniel. (See: Norman O. Brown, "Metamorphosis II: Actaeon," in: *The American Poetry Review*, I,1 [November/December, 1972], 38ff.) Brown's Freudian perspective also suggests a relation between the image of Odysseus and the Cyclops, on the one hand, and coitus and masturbation, on the other. A giant with an eye (urethra) in the center of the head (penis) enters a cave (vagina) and, in the end, blocks the door. Or, put differently, Odysseus' pointed ram-rod with its fiery end breaks the membrane of Polyphemos and enters him at the center. One might recall in this regard the folkloric connection made between male masturbation and blindness.

11. On the theme of the poet's task in a time of dearth, see: Martin Heidegger, *Existence and Being* (Chicago: Gateway, 1949), especially the two essays on the poetry of Friedrich Hölderlin. Also see: Heidegger, *Poetry, Language, Thought* (New York: Harper and Row, 1971); and Stanley Romaine Hopper, "On the Naming of the Gods in Hölderlin and Rilke," in: Michalson, ed., *Christianity and the Existentialists* (New York: Scribners, 1956), pp. 148–190.

12. Euripides' strategy is to link the story of Dionysos' capture by the Lydian pirates (see: *The Homeric Hymn to Dionysos*) with the Odysseus/Polyphemos episode from *The Odyssey*. Silenos becomes the clue to the connection since he is the traditional tutor of Dionysos and, in Euripides' telling of it, the servant of Polyphemos.

13. This is William Arrowsmith's felicitous characterization. See: Grene and Lattimore, eds., *The Complete Greek Tragedies, Volume III: Euripides* (Chicago: University of Chicago Press, 1959), p. 228.

14. Theocritus, *Idylls*, IX.34. Compare: *Idylls*, XI.25–27; and Virgil, *Eclogue*, II, and VIII.38–43.

15. Tom Jones, *The Fantasticks* (New York: Drama Books, 1964), p. 28.

16. Heraclitus, frag. #107 (Diels-Kranz numbering).

17. Joyce Cary, *The Horse's Mouth* (New York: Harper and Row, 1965), p. 108.

18. W. H. Roscher, *Lexicon der Grieschen und Römischen Mythologie* (Hildesheim: Olms, 1965), Vol. III, pt. 2, pp. 2698ff. Compare: *The Odyssey*, 1.71ff; *Theogony*, 143; Apollodorus, I.1–7.

19. See: Job 38:1; 42:5.

20. Marie-Louise von Franz links psychological difficulties of the "eye" and the putting out of Polyphemos eye, on the one hand, with David, the shepherd boy, putting out the eye of Goliath the Giant, in:

Aurora Consurgens (New York: Pantheon, 1966), p. 382; compare Jung's discussion of the "eye" as "devouring female darkness," as for example in Song of Solomon 4:9 (see: *CW*, XIV.24). It might be possible to think of a tic in an eye as a physical symptom of what could be called "the Cyclops syndrome." Characteristics of this syndrome would be a compulsion to perfection in behavior, a mimetic attitude in personal vocation and social relationships, and a rational ego-consciousness in value judgments. The body-language in this case would be indicating a "wish" to put out the ego-eye so that a deeper way of "seeing" might be gained; or, the tic itself might be interpreted as the suffering of the putting out of the eye, in which instance it would be important to read the cycloptic meaning of the suffering rather than to wish to overcome the symptom too quickly or easily. Western culture has perhaps suffered "the Cyclops syndrome" collectively, the twentieth century being a "tic" in the eye of the culture's egoism, its historical rational consciousness.

21. John 9:39.

22. For an account of the relation of the children's game to Jesus' Passion, see: David L. Miller, *"Empaidzein:* Playing the Mock Game (Luke 22:63–64)," in: *Journal of Biblical Literature*, XC, III (1971), 309ff.

23. Polyphemos' name is itself to the point of the Gospels concerning Pharasaic literalism, that is, the point against seeing with single vision. The root of the name, Polyphemos, is *phymidzō*, and it means "prophesy," "promise," or "report." But the word implies a special sort of "saying," a *phēmē. The Odyssey* calls it an utterance prompted by the gods (*Odyssey*, II.35; XX.100). Herodotus says that such utterances ("prophetic" here meaning "forth-telling" rather than "fore-telling") often come from dreams (Herodotus I.43). The prefix of the Cyclops' name, *poly-,* means "much" or "many." A usual interpretation of "Polyphemos" is therefore "famous" or "spoken of much." But the special quality of the root implies something more. It connotes the plurality of divine utterances of the sort that come by dream, coming as they do from the cavern of the wounded eye, from a grotesque and freakish polymorphous perversity, a many-sidedness of dream's deep night-seeing, visions from an underworld nothing of ego's nobody.

24. *Metamorphosis,* 259; compare, Roscher, *op. cit.,* Vol. II. pt. 1, pp. 1675ff.

25. Apollodorus, III.122.

26. For the development of this motif, see: Theodor H. Gaster, *Myth, Legend, and Custom in the Old Testament* (New York: Harper and Row, 1969), pp. 51ff. The theme of the war between two brothers is also treated in: Alan Watts, *The Two Hands of God* (New York: Braziller, 1963), pp. 113–146. Watts deals especially with Horus/Set, Kamatha/Marubhūti, Jacob/Esau, the Prodigal Son/Elder Brother, Ahura Mazda/Angra Mainu, in addition to Cain/Abel.

27. See: David Williams, "Aspects du role mediateur des monstres," *Sciences religieuses*, VI, 3 (1976–77), 268. This author also discusses the monstrous genitalia, associating the nature of the polyphemic body with the hermetic soul of the ram.

28. Mircea Eliade, *Shamanism* (New York: Pantheon, 1964), p. 470.

29. Gaster, *loc. cit.*

30. See: David L. Miller, "Homo Religiousus and the Death of God," in: *Journal of Bible and Religion*, XXXIV, 4 (October, 1966), 305ff.

31. Plato, *The Laws*, 680b; and Aristotle, *Nicho. Ethics*, X.9. Compare: Werner Jaeger, *Paideia: The Ideals of Greek Culture*, trans. G. Highet (New York: Oxford, 1944), Vol. III, p. 232.

32. *The Book of Enoch*, 85–91.

33. See page 12, above.

34. Georges Duplian, "On the Frontiers of Knowledge: An Interview with C. G. Jung," in: *Spring 1960* (Dallas), 8.

35. I Corinthians 1:25.

36. Erasmus, *Ten Colloquies*, trans. Thompson (Indianapolis: Library of Liberal Arts, 1957), pp. 121, 124, where also, speaking of Polyphemos' drinking, Cannius says: ". . . you take a long drink . . . your whole body glows; your face turns rosy; your expression grows merry. . . . The Gospel has the same effect when it penetrates the heart. It makes a new man of you."

8 Shepherd and Clown

1. The relationship of Silenos and Polyphemos has been established by way of Euripides' play in the last chapter. On the connection between Hermes and Silenos, see: Kerényi, *op. cit.*, pp. 88f. Also, see Part III of this book for more explicit argument of the relationship between the themes of Silenos and Christ.

2. John H. Towsen, *Clowns* (New York: Hawthorn, 1976), Chapter I; William Willeford, *The Fool and his Scepter* (Evanston: Northwestern University Press, 1969), p. 11 and *passim*. See also: Enid Welsford, *The Fool* (Garden City: Doubleday, 1961). Martin Grotjahn has shown the obscene, phallic nature of clowns and the comic, in: *Beyond Laughter* (New York: McGraw-Hill/Blakiston, 1957).

3. Towsen, *op. cit.*, p. 25.

4. Ibid., p. 22. On the grotesque, see: Williams, *op. cit.*, 267ff; and Georges Canguilhem, "Monstrosity and the Monstrous," in: *Diogenes,* XL (Winter, 1962), 27f. Canguilhem implies that there is a strong link between monster and clown; for example, he speaks of "the creators of human monsters destined to be clowns, as described by Victor Hugo in *L'Homme qui rit*" (p. 40). He also discusses the relation between the concept of the monstrous and Gaston Bachelard's notion of the imaginal as the "deformational work." Canguilhem writes: "The power of the imagination is inexhaustible, indefatigable. . . . In this way we see that the monstrous, inasmuch as it is imaginary, proliferates" (p. 41). See also: Rafael Lopez-Pedraza, *Hermes and his Children* (Dallas: Spring Publications, 1978), especially the section on Priapos; and Leslie Fiedler, *Freaks: Myths and Images of the Secret Self* (New York: Simon and Schuster, 1978).

5. Willeford, *op. cit.*, p. 66. This quotation appears in a chapter on "The Fool and Mimesis." From the perspective of this book, Willeford takes too literally the clown's mirror, or the clown as mirror, not noticing it to be a magic mirror which does not reflect things as they literally are, but distorts them, like Picasso says of art, so that they may be the lie which tells the truth. The clownish mirror does not mirror (Willeford's own examples bear this out!); it does not have a mimetic, *imitatio* nature. Rather, the clown's magic mirroring is *poïēsis*. His art is poetry. It allows us to see just what the external, serious, literal eye cannot.

6. Ibid., p. 28. Compare this author's earlier essay which argues for the figure of the clown, not precisely as an image of imperfection, but rather as the image of failure: "Playing the Game to Lose," in: J. Moltmann, ed., *Theology of Play* (New York: Harper and Row, 1972), pp. 99–110. For further discussion of the relation between fool and prophet, especially the Arabic instance of the fool as *sha'ir*, "poet-seer," see: Welsford, *op. cit.*, p. 79 and *passim.*

7. *As You Like It*, II.iv.66. Alex Aronson has discussed at length the relation between the character of the fool in Shakespeare and the notion of "seeing" and "blindness." He notes a connection between *eros* and blindness not unlike the silenic link between Hermes' ram and Polyphemos' lost sight. See: *Psyche and Symbol in Shakespeare* (Bloomington: Indiana University Press, 1972), pp. 26f, 86f, 139f, and 325, ftn. 12).

8. The monstrous-grotesque, the shepherd and clown are juxtaposed in a well-known passage in which Friedrich Nietzsche is calling attention to the importance of restoring a Dionysian sense of the Greek satyr/shepherd to later idyllic Christianity, the former possessing a "traumatically wounded vision" as over against some "tender, fluting" image. (See: Nietzsche, *The Birth of Tragedy* [Garden City: Doubleday, 1956], pp. 52ff.) The passage involves a grotesque vision of Zarathustra seeing a shepherd biting off the head of a serpent which he cannot subsequently swallow. At the end of the vision this shepherd is viewed as a sort of clown. The text reads: "Far away he spewed the head of the snake—and he jumped up. No longer shepherd, no longer human—one changed, radiant, *laughing!* Never yet on earth has a human being laughed as he laughed! O my brothers, I heard a laughter that was no human laughter; and now a thirst gnaws at me, a longing that never grows still. My longing for this laughter gnaws at me; oh, how do I bear to go on living! And how could I bear to die now!" (*Thus Spoke Zarathustra* [New York: Viking, 1966], pp. 159f.) This is the same Zarathustra who sings, "Hating all lamb souls, / Grimly hating whatever looks / Sheepish, lamb-eyed, curly-wooled, / Gray, with lambs' and sheeps' goodwill. . . . You that have seen man / As god and sheep: / Tearing to pieces the god in man / No less than the sheep in man, / And laughing while tearing" (ibid., pp. 299f). Note Jung's treatment of this passage by Nietzsche, in: *CW*, V.586.

9. See Part Two of this book, pp. 66 & 96. Also: Wolfgang Zucker, "The Image of the Clown," in: *Journal of Aesthetics and Art Criticism*, III, 12 (March, 1954); and compare, Zucker, "The Clown as the Lord of Disorder," in: *Theology Today*, XXIV, 3 (October, 1967), 306ff. For more material on this theme, see the materials mentioned in footnote #2, above. A more recent manifestation of the same warring brotherhood is in a song entitled, "The Farmer and the Cowboy," from the musical, *Oklahoma*. And, see: Alan Watts, *The Two Hands of God* (New York: Braziller, 1963).

10. T. S. Eliot, *The Complete Poems and Plays* (New York: Harcourt Brace Jovanovich, 1952), pp. 309f.

11. Ibid., pp. 365, 348, 354, 307, 310, 378.

12. "Ordinary Evening in New Haven, XXI," in: *The Collected Poems* (New York: Knopf, 1975), p. 480.

13. "The Old Lutheran Bells at Home," ibid., p. 461.

14. Ibid., p. 400. Compare: Lopez-Pedraza, *loc. cit.*

15. See: Aeschylus, *Agamemnon*. 718–736.

16. James Dickey, *Poems 1957–1967* (Middletown: Wesleyan University Press, 1967), pp. 252f.

17. Sidney Alberts, *A Bibliography of the Works of Robinson Jeffers* (New York, 1933), pp. 56–57. Compare: Robinson Jeffers, *Dear Judas and Other Poems* (New York: Liveright, 1977), p. 132.

18. Ibid.

19. Ibid., p. 114. Also notice the theme of the single eye in the figure of the horse and of Vasquez in this poem.

20. Compare the treatment of the Shepherd/Sheep image in: Robert Pirsig, *Zen and the Art of Motorcycle Maintenance* (New York: Bantam, 1975), pp. 386ff: "Quality for sheep is what the shepherd says. And if you take a sheep and put it up at the timberline at night when the wind is roaring, that sheep will be panicked half to death and will call and call until the shepherd comes, or comes the wolf. ... But Phaedrus is no shepherd either and the strain of behaving like one is killing him. A strange thing that has always occurred in classes occurs again, when the unruly and wild students in the back rows have always empathized with him and been his favorites, while the more sheepish and obedient students in the front rows have always been terrorized by him and are because of this objects of his contempt, even though in the end the sheep have passed and his unruly friends in the back rows have not. And Phaedrus sees, though he does not want to admit it to himself even now, he sees intuitively nevertheless that his days as a shepherd are coming to an end too. And he wonders more and more what is going to happen next."

21. "The Owl in the Sarcophagus," *op. cit.*, p. 434. Compare Stevens' treatment of Crispin, the "comedian as the letter C," who is "an introspective voyager" and whose "eye most apt in gelatines and jupes" is not unlike that of the blinded Cyclops. (Ibid., pp. 27ff).

22. Theodore Roethke, *The Collected Poems* (New York: Doubleday, 1975), p. 236.

9 Clown and Christ

1. Harvey Cox, *The Feast of Fools* (Cambridge: Harvard University Press, 1969), p. 140.

2. Jaraslov Pelikan, *Fools for Christ* (Philadelphia: Muhlenberg, 1955).

3. Walter Nigg, *Der christliche Narr* (Zürich: Artemis Verlag, 1956).

4. Lesek Kolakowski, "The Priest and the Jester," in: *Dissent*, IX, 3 (Summer, 1962), 233.

5. (New York: Harper and Row, 1964).

6. (Richmond: John Knox Press, 1966); compare, Vos, *For God's Sake Laugh!* (Richmond: John Knox Press, 1967).

7. (Richmond: John Knox Press, 1970).

8. (Battle Creek: Ellis, 1901).

9. (New York: Seabury Press, 1969); compare, Hyers, "The Recovery of Simplicity," in: *Christian Century*, (August 7, 1974), 768–771.

10. Robert Funk, *Language, Hermeneutic, and Word of God* (New York: Harper and Row, 1966), Part II; Dan O. Via, *Kerygma and Comedy in the New Testament* (Philadelphia: Fortress Press, 1975), pp. 39–70; and, John Dominic Crossan, *Raid on the Articulate: Comic Eschatology in Jesus and Borges* (New York: Harper and Row, 1976), *passim*.

11. Geo Widengren, "Harlenkintracht und Mönchskutte, Clownhut und Derwischmütze," in: *Orientalia suecana*, II (1953), 41–111.

12. Cox, *The Seduction of the Spirit* (New York: Simon and Schuster, 1973), final page.

13. Lawrence Durrell, *Clea* (New York: Pocket Books, 1961), pp. 133ff. Compare James Joyce's request: "Write me your essayes, my vocational scholars, but corsorily dipping your noses in it." [*Finnegans Wake* (New York: Viking, 1939), p. 447.]

14. Tom Robbins, *Another Roadside Attraction* (New York: Ballantine, 1971), p. 298.

15. Ibid., p. 301.

16. Ibid.

17. Wallace Stevens, "The Comedian as the Letter C," in: *The Collected Poems* (New York: Knopf, 1975), p. 36.

18. Ibid., p. 39.

19. Friedrich Nietzsche, Grossoktav, WW XI, 20, cited in: Martin Heidegger, "The Nature of Language," *On the Way to Language*, trans. Hertz (New York: Harper and Row, 1971), p. 70. Heidegger's essay was originally delivered as a lecture in the *studium generale* of the University of Freiburg im Bresgau on 4 December 1957, and was later published under the title, *Unterwegs zur Sprache* (1959).

20. Alan Watts, "Do You Smell?" *Alan Watts Journal*, I.12 (October, 1970), p. 1.

10 The Image of the Clown and Smell's Drunk Sense

1. Heinrich Böll, *The Clown*, trans. Vennewitz (New York: Avon, 1975), p. 13.

2. Ibid.

3. Ibid., p. 30.

4. Ibid., p. 34.

5. Ibid., p. 63.

6. Ibid., p. 172.

7. Ibid., p. 174.

8. Ibid., p. 11.

9. Ibid., p. 10.

10. Ibid., p. 94.

11. Ibid., p. 125.

12. William Blake, "Night the Ninth, being the Last Judgment, from 'The Four Zoas,'" in: *Selected Poetry-Prose of William Blake*, ed. Frye (New York: Modern Library, 1953), pp. 238f.

11 A Red Nose on White: The Clown's Archetypal Face

1. For particulars of this history, see: John H. Towsen, *Clowns* (New York: Hawthorn, 1976); and Laurence Senelick, *Cavalcade of Clowns* (San Francisco: Bellerophon, 1977).

2. Towsen, *op. cit.*, pp. 4, 32, 96, 134, 184, 211, 238ff, 369, 371.

3. A. B. Keith, *The Sanskrit Drama* (London: Oxford, 1924), p. 108. Compare: Towsen, *op. cit.*, pp. 32, 359 ftn. 1.

4. Cited in: F. O. Matthiesson, *American Renaissance* (New York: Oxford, 1941), p. 204.

5. Virgil, *Eclogue*, VI.14–22. The term used by Virgil, *sanguineis*, is from *sanguis*, which means "bloody" and "blood-colored," as in the color of wine (compare Pliny, XIV.ix.11) or as the moisture of fruit-juice (compare Pliny, XXI.xvi.56). The term also refers to "vigor," "life," "force," and "spirit."

12 Nasal Fantasia, 1: Psychology

1. Cited in: Sigmund Freud, *The Origins of Psychoanalysis: Letters to Wilhelm Fliess*, trans. Mosbacher and Strachey (New York: Basic Books, 1954), p. 5.

2. Ibid., pp. 121, 74 ftn.

3. Otto Fenichel, "The Long Nose," *Collected Papers* (New York: Norton, 1953), pp. 155ff.

4. Compare the report which Jacques Lacan gives of one of Freud's cases which the latter tells about in an article on "fetishism" from 1927. In order to achieve sexual satisfaction the patient needed something shining on his partner's nose (in German: *Glanz auf der Nase*). Analysis revealed that in earlier English-speaking years this man had had a burning curiosity about the "phallus of his mother." In due course this curiosity had been repressed. Pronouncing the patient's fetish in English revealed the repressed wish (*Glanz auf der Nase* = "glance at her 'nose'"). See: Lacan, "The Insistence of the Letter in the Unconscious," in: Ehrmann, ed., *Structuralism* (Garden City: Anchor Books, 1970), p. 131.

5. Marie-Louise von Franz, *Shadow and Evil in Fairy Tales* (Dallas: Spring Publications, 1974), pp. 51f. It might also be noted that one meaning of the vernacular verb, "to nose," is "to spy," hence, the private eye, the spy, turns out to be a "nose"! Or, one might say that the nose, the intuition, is one's *private* "eye," one's undercover or underworld way of seeing.

6. See: A. Wünsche, *Der Sagenkreis vom Geprellten* (Leipzig: 1905), pp. 84f

7. Also, hyenas can smell food up to ten kilometers, and butterflies can smell each other for purposes of mating up to eleven kilometers! See: "The World of Smell," in: Huygen and Portvliet, *Gnomes* (New York: Abrams, 1977), p. 24 (unnumbered).

13 Nasal Fantasia, 2: Literature

1. James Joyce, *Finnegans Wake* (New York: Viking, 1939), pp. 95f.
2. Ibid., p. 133.
3. Ibid., p. 322.
4. Ibid., pp. 378f.
5. Ibid., p. 579.
6. Laurence Sterne, *Tristram Shandy* (New York: Signet, 1962), p. 176.
7. Ibid., p. 185.
8. Ibid.
9. Ibid., p. 186.
10. Ibid., p. 172.
11. Ibid., p. 52.
12. Ibid., p. 173.
13. Ibid., p. 207.
14. Ibid., p. 201.
15. Ibid., p. 218.
16. Ibid., p. 189.
17. See: William W. Rowe, *Through Gogol's Looking Glass: Reverse Vision, False Focus, and Precarious Logic* (New York: New York University Press, 1976), pp. 100–106; and Ivan Yermakov, "The Nose," in: Robert Maguire, ed., *Gogol from the Twentieth Century* (Princeton: Princeton University Press, 1974), pp. 155–198.

18. A similar point about metaphoric, as opposed to literal, ways of thinking and feeling is made, utilizing the image of the nose, by William Gass, in an essay entitled, "Carrots, Noses, Snow, Rose, Roses" (see: Gass, *The World within the Word* (New York: Knopf, 1978), pp. 180–307). Gass is speaking about the "ontological transformation" that

takes place in the language of poetry and he gives a snowman as an example. "The snow that makes up the snowman remains snow, though it has also become body—snowbody, one must hesitate to say—but the coals alter absolutely. They are buttons or eyes. Because of its natural shape and the new relations it has entered, the carrot does not simply stand for or resemble a nose, *it literally is a nose now*—the nose of a specific snowman. Several characteristics, which were central to its definition as a carrot, carry on. Its slim funnular form is certainly suitable, and we can pretend that orange is red in order to imagine that the nose is cold . . . uncomfortable and runny. . . . a carrot will clearly work better as a nose than a jelly spoon or toilet tube. . . . if I succeeded in impressing my work with inner worth the way Yeats did his symbol system, you would have to be reminded that it was not snownoses that were being served for dinner alongside the roast. . . . The carrot does not name a nose. It is one." (Ibid., pp. 288f, 297, 299.)

14   The Smell of Traditional Religion & its Mythic Under-odor

1. *Temple Bar*, V.524.

2. II Corinthians 2:14–16.

3. For example: Leviticus 1:9, 13, 17; 2:2, 9, 12; etc., and, Numbers 15:3, 7, 10, 13, 14, 24; etc.

4. Tor Andrae, *Mohammed: The Man and His Faith*, tr. Theophile Menzel (Freeport, N.Y.: Books for Libraries Press, 1971), p. 109.

5. Philo, *On Dreams*, I.41–42, 47–49, 51.

6. Psalm 115:6. Compare the notion of *vāsanā* in the Yogācāra School of Mahayana Buddhism. The Sanskrit word is based on the root, *vas-*, meaning, "to dwell" or "to abide." But in the religious context it indicates the "smell" which *abides* or *lives* in a piece of cloth which has been incensed. More particularly, *vāsanā* is the unconscious tendency by which the so-called "subtle body" is "perfumed" or "fragranced," and it refers to a function of the deepest self which leaves an aroma of its spiritual wisdom (*ālaya vijñāna*). On this matter, see: Toshihiko Izutzu, "The Field Structure of Time in Zen Buddhism," *Eranos 47–1978* (Surkampf Verlag, forthcoming); and Heinrich Zimmer, *Philosophies of India,* ed. Campbell (New York: Meridian, 1956), pp. 324, 526.

7. Cited in: *Oxford English Dictionary, op. cit.,* I.1975.

8. Cited in: Ibid. Not only does iniquity stink, but even sanctity can have a bad odor. For example, note the saying of Zen: "*Miso* ('bean paste') with the smell of *miso* is not good *miso*. Enlightenment with a smell of enlightenment is not the real enlightenment." (Zenkei Shibayama, *A Flower Does Not Talk*, trans. Kudo [Rutland: Charles Tuttle, 1970], p. 196.)

9. Aeschylus, *Agamemnon*, 1095, 1185, 1307ff.

10. See: Claude Lévi-Strauss, *The Raw and the Cooked* (Introduction to a Science of Mythology, Volume I), trans. Weightman and Weightman (New York: Harper and Row, 1969), p. 154.

11. See: ibid., p. 155.

12. See: ibid., pp. 154ff, 161, 176–179, 249–251.

13. Euripides, *Hippolytus*, 1391ff: "O divine fragrance! Even in my pain / I sense it, and the suffering is lightened. / The goddess Artemis is near this place." Compare the saying in *The Acts of Thomas* from the New Testament Apocrypha: the Queen "flows with all delicious unguent," that is, a sweet smell comes from the goddess. (Cited in: Jung, *CW*, XIV.498.)

14. See: "The Hymns of Orpheus," in: Raine and Harper, eds., *Thomas Taylor the Platonist* (Princeton: Princeton University Press, 1969), pp. 209–293.

15. See: *The Holy Bible*, eds. May and Metzger (New York: Oxford, 1962), p. 1008 ftn.

16. H. W. F. Saggs, "The Branch to the Nose," *Journal of Theological Studies*, New Series XI (1960), pp. 320, 323.

17. Ibid., pp. 324f.

18. Ibid., p. 326.

15 Moistening: The Humor of our Wits' End

1. See: Ben Jonson, *Every Man out of his Humour* (1599); also, David Miller, "Achelous and the Butterfly," *Spring 1973* (Dallas), 1–23; and, Paracelsus, *Hermetic and Alchemical Writings*, ed. Waite (Berkeley: Shambala, 1976), Volume II, pp. 124–127.

2. Compare: Stuart M. Tave, *The Amiable Humorist* (Chicago: University of Chicago Press, 1960), p. 227.

3. Cited in: ibid., p. 230.

4. Cited in: ibid., p. 111.

5. Cited in: ibid., p. 236.

6. *Comedy of Errors*, V.i.86.

7. *King Lear*, III.iv.58.

8. *Merry Wives of Windsor*, IV.v.100.

9. *Comedy of Errors*, V.i.96.

10. *Timon of Athens,* IV.iii.89.

11. *Twelfth Night,* IV.ii.95.

12. *Oxford English Dictionary, op. cit.,* II.3796.

13. Stephen Hawes, *The Pastime of Pleasure,* XXIV.2. I have taken the liberty of changing two of Hawes' phrases: "common wit" to "common sense," and "estimation" to "conjecture." This has been done only to make better modern sense of terms whose archaic meanings are somewhat misleading in today's speech. Compare: Albertus Magnus, *De anima,* where *vis aestimativa* is equivalent to "wit," especially to what he calls "inner wit." On this, see: C. S. Lewis, *The Discarded Image* (Cambridge: At the University Press, 1964), pp. 162f; and Lewis, *Studies in Words* (Cambridge: At the University Press, 1960), pp. 86–110, 147–148.

14. *Much Ado about Nothing,* V.iv.99. Compare: William Congreve, "Concerning Humour in Comedy" (a letter to John Dennis), cited in: Paul Lauter, ed., *Theories of Comedy* (Garden City: Doubleday, 1964), pp. 219, 209.

15. Cited in: Tave, *op. cit.,* p. 220.

16. John Dennis, "A Large Account of the Taste in Poetry, and the Causes of the Degeneracy of It," cited in: Lauter, *op. cit.,* p. 219.

17. Cited in: ibid., p. 220. On this perspective, see: Tave, *op. cit.,* p. viii.

18. Cited in: ibid., p. 106.

19. John Trusler, *The Distinction between Words Esteemed Synonymous,* cited in: ibid., p. 266, ftn. 22.

20. William Hazlitt, *Lectures on the Comic Writers, Etc. of Great Britain* (1819); and John Locke, *Essay Concerning Human Understanding,* II.xi.2. These are both cited in: Lauter, *op. cit.,* pp. 262ff, 279 ftn. 2.

21. Many have commented on what we all know: how wit devoid of humor can be sharp and dry. We say, "cutting." See, for example, Tilloston's remarks, cited by Tave, *op. cit.,* pp. 13, 14, 22. There is also the view of the psychoanalyst, Martin Grotjahn, concerning the wit-type person: "The wit as such is hostile, often with a skillful, artful, highly developed, sophisticated meanness and viciousness. He nurses and polishes his meanness like Narcissus himself seeking to sparkle with brilliance in the mirror." (*Beyond Laughter* [New York: McGraw-Hill, 1957], p. 44.)

22. Joyce, *op. cit.,* p. 154. The German language manifests the link between "wit" and "smell" which is being indicated here by Joyce's word, "nase." The term for "wit" in German, *Witz,* belongs to the

language-group that includes *wissen,* meaning "to know," and *wittern,* meaning "to smell out" (compare *witterung,* referring to "weather" or "atmospheric conditions," and *Gewitterdaemonen,* about which we have already commented on p. 38, above.

16 Warming: A Phenomenology of Straight and Round

1. Cited in: Gaston Bachelard, *The Poetics of Space,* trans. Jolas (New York: Orion, 1964), p. 232.
2. Ibid.
3. Ibid.
4. Ibid., p. 237.
5. Ibid., pp 239f. The translation here is from Rilke's *Poèmes français.* Compare: Lu Pu-wei, *Frühling und Herbst,* trans. Wilhelm (Jena, 1928), p. 38: "Heaven's way is round, earth's way is square."
6. Stevens, *op. cit.,* p. 76.
7. Plato, *The Phaedo,* 108.
8. Jung, *CW,* XII.6. Compare paragraph #172 in the same volume where Jung notes that in ancient times the god Hermes was both *stroggulos kai tetragōnos* ("round and square").
9. Delmore Schwartz, *Selected Poems: Summer Knowledge* (New York: New Directions, 1967), pp. 157, 158.

17 The Red and the White: A Clown's Nasal Alchemy

1. See: J. E. Cirlot, *A Dictionary of Symbols* (New York: Philosophical Library, 1962), p. 57.
2. See the saying of C. G. Jung: "The alchemists had keen noses," in: *CW,* XVI.353.
3. See: Jung, *CW* XII.333f.
4. Jung, *CW,* XIV.7.
5. Jung, *CW,* XII.334. Often in alchemy the goal of the *opus* is the uniting of "red and white sulfur," of "the red man and the white woman," of *"Venus alba et rubea,"* or of "Sun and Moon." See: Jung, *CW,* XIV.634f, 720. For a slightly different view of the *rubedo/albedo* complex, see: Marie-Louise von Franz, ed., *Aurora consurgens,* trans. Hull and Glover (New York: Pantheon, 1966), p. 206. Also: concerning the sun-as-red and the moon-as-white uniting in relation to a sense of "smell," note the saying at the end of the Nag Hammadi Book of Thomas the Contender: "The sun and the moon will give fragrance to

you" (in: *The Nag Hammadi Library in English* [New York: Harper and Row, 1977], p. 194.).

6. Friedrich Nietzsche, *Thus Spoke Zarathustra*, trans. Kaufmann (New York: Viking, 1966), p. 321.

7. Malachi 4:2a.

18 Fullness and Time

1. Oribasius, VIII.xxxv.7. This man was the physician to Julian in the fourth century of the Common Era, but his use of *plēroma* is a commonplace in the classical world.

2. Plutarch, *Lysander*, XIX.

3. Herodotus, III.67.

4. Aristotle, Metaphysics, 988[a]; also, *Historia animalium*, 57.

5. Aeschylus, *Seven Against Thebes*, 464.

6. Sophocles, *Philoctetes*, 324; Euripides, *Hippolytus*, 1328.

7. Plato, *Gorgias*, 496[e].

8. Euripides, *The Cyclops*, 209; *Ion*, 1051, 1170; *Iphigenia at Taurus*, 954.

9. Matthew 8:19, 12:38; 19:16; 22:16, 24, 36; Mark 4:38; 9:17, 38; 10:17, 20, 35; 12:14, 19, 32; 13:1; Luke 3:12; 7:40; 9:38; 10:25; 1:45; 12:13; 18:18; 19:39; 20:21, 39; 21:7; John 8:4; 20:16; etc. There are actually 58 occurrences of the word, "teacher" (*didaskolos*) in the New Testament. Of these, 48 are in the Gospels and 41 of these refer to Jesus. Direct address accounts for 29 of the 41 instances.

10. Mark 10:17; Luke 18:18.

11. Justin Martyr, *Apology*, I.13 (compare, 1.4, 12, 13, 21, etc.).

19 Teaching/Preaching: An Inside/Outside Split

1. J. N. Sanders, *Foundations of the Christian Faith* (New York: Philosophical Library, 1952), pp. 30, 32.

2. Emil Brunner, *The Mediator: A Study of the Central Doctrine of the Christian Faith* (Philadelphia: Westminster, 1947), pp. 417, 418, 420.

3. Karl Barth, *The Doctrine of the Word of God* (Prolegomena to a Church Dogmatics, Volume I, Part I) (Edinburgh: Clark, 1936), pp. 55, 97. Compare these words of the historian of religions, G. Van der Leeuw: "The teacher . . . is to be distinguished from the preacher by the fading element of Power in the word. . . . he is generally less

important personally; for he neither imparts salvation nor announces it, but merely speaks about it." (*Religion in Essence and Manifestation* [New York: Harper and Row, 1963], Volume I, p. 228.)

4. Mark 1:14.

5. Matthew 10:7. The so-called "Great Commission" in Matthew 28:19-20 ("Go therefore . . . teaching . . .") refers to the work *after* the people have already been converted by the primary preaching, or so goes the standard theological interpretation.

6. See: Gerhard Kittel, ed., *Theological Dictionary of the New Testament,* trans. G. Bromiley (Grand Rapids: Eerdmans, 1965), Volume III, pp. 683–717. For an example of a reputable contemporary scholar who persists in this view, see: Norman Perrin, *The New Testament: An Introduction* (New York: Harcourt Brace Jovanovich, 1974), pp. 174ff.

7. Matthew 7:29; Mark 1:22; compare Luke 4:16–30. The term for "authority" here is *exousian,* meaning literally, "out of the essence," or "out of the substance." The suggestion seems to be that "authoritative" teaching has *body* in it.

8. Aristophanes' play is *The Clouds.* Philip Roth's novel is *Professor of Desire.* Wallace Stevens' poem is "Ordinary Evening in New Haven." The reader will think of many other examples in literature, opera, and painting.

9. Kittel, ed., *op. cit.,* vol. III, pp. 683, 695.

10. *Iliad,* II.50, 442; IX.10; XXIII.39; *Odyssey,* II.6; Aristotle, *Politics,* VII.4; Demosthenes, *Orations,* XII.4. Compare: Kittel, ed., *op. cit.,* vol. II, p. 687.

11. Luke 12:3.

12. Kittel, ed., *op. cit.,* vol. III, p. 708.

13. See: Kittel, ed., *op. cit.,* vol. II, p. 139.

14. The formula, "faith seeking understanding," is that of Anselm. It is the classical definition of theological teaching, see: Introduction, p. xx. For the *gnosis/pistis* ("knowledge/faith") distinction, see: Barth, *op. cit.,* p. 92.

15. Matthew 23:3.

20 Making Outer Inner: The Two as One

1. Robert Grant, *A Historical Introduction to the New Testament* (New York: Harper and Row, 1963), pp. 81ff (italics added).

2. See: Kittel, ed., *op. cit.,* vol. II, p. 139; vol. III, p. 713. Also: Josef Blinzer, "Jesus and his Disciples," in: H. J. Schultz, ed., *Jesus in his*

Time (Philadelphia: Fortress Press, 1971), pp. 86ff.

3. For example, see: Perrin, *op. cit.*, p. 295.

4. *The Gospel according to Thomas* (New York: Harper and Row, 1959), logion 22.

21 From Socrates to Silenos: Remythologizing the Image of the Teacher

1. Compare Blinzer, *op. cit.*, pp. 84ff. Blinzer here is puzzling over the meaning of the Greek term for "disciple," *mathētēs*. His point is: "Unlike the classical Greek and Hellenistic world . . . The Old Testament does not know a master-disciple relationship. Neither the writings of the prophets nor those of the scribes of the Old Testament contain any such idea" (p. 85).

2. Compare the work of Paul Elmer More, and see Gilson's book, *The Spirit of Medieval Philosophy*.

3. In: Soren Kierkegaard, *The Concept of Irony, with Constant Reference to Socrates*, trans. Capel (New York: Harper and Row, 1966), p. 401, ftn. 12.

4. Ibid., *passim.* esp. pp. 241f, ftn., and 401, ftn. 12; Karl Jaspers, *Socrates, Buddha, Confucius, Jesus* (from: The Great Philosophers, Vol. I), ed. Arendt (New York: Harvest Books, 1962), esp. pp. 87ff (for Jaspers, Socrates and Christ are "paradigmatic individuals" of Great Teaching); and Stanley Romaine Hopper, *The Crisis of Faith* (Nashville: Abingdon Press, 1944), Chap. IV: "Christian Socratism."

5. Compare: Hopper, *op. cit.*, pp. 263ff, where this argument is explained in detail.

6. Epictetus, *Discourses*, I.29.46f; III.1.36f; 13.9ff; 21.13ff; 22.46ff.

7. James Hillman, "On Psychological Creativity," *Eranos* 35–1966 (Zürich: Rhein Verlag, 1969), pp. 370–398; compare, Hillman, *The Myth of Analysis* (Evanston: Northwestern University Press, 1972), pp. 72–78; and Pierre Hadot, "La Figure de Socrate," *Eranos 43–1974* (Leiden: Brill, 1977), pp. 51–90.

8. Plato, *Symposium*, 215–221.

9. Justin Martyr, *Apology*, I.21–22.

10. See Kittel's reference to Aristophanes' play, *The Birds*, and the connection to later Christian notions of Teacher, in: *op. cit.*, vol. II, p. 149.

11. Silenos has already been mentioned in this book. See pages 37, 45, 68. His function in those places was as friend of Polyphemos, the monstrous shepherd, and as prototype of the clown, especially in his

drunkenness. In the chapters which follow, the silenic connection to Christ will be more explicitly drawn, though this god has, as it were, presided over the meditations from the beginning. His emptiness and his cave, along with the person and work of Christ, link the three separate parts of the book.

22 Silenos and Christ: The True Vine as the Great Teacher

1. Virgil, *Eclogue,* VI.14f.
2. Ibid.; and, Aelian, *Varia historia,* III.18.
3. Pausanius, *Guide to Greece,* I.iv.5; compare, Euripides, *The Cyclops, passim.*
4. Apollodorus, *Library,* II.83ff.
5. Karl Kerényi, *The Religion of the Greeks and Romans* (New York: Dutton, 1962), p. 195.
6. *Orphica,* 53 (54).
7. Karl Kerényi, "Man and Masks," *Eranos 16–1948,* in: Campbell, ed., *Spiritual Disciplines* (Papers from the Eranos Yearbooks, Vol. IV) (New York: Pantheon, 1960), p. 160.
8. Plutarch, *Moralia* ("Letter to Apollonius"), 115B–D.
9. Walter Otto, *Dionysos: Myth and Cult,* trans. Palmer (Bloomington: Indiana University Press, 1965), p. 177.
10. Aeschylus, *Agamemnon,* 740; Euripides, *Bacchae,* 115; Plato, *Theaetetus,* 153ᶜ.
11. Plutarch, *Moralia, loc. cit.*
12. Erwin Rhode, *Psyche* (New York: Harper and Row, 1966), Volume II, p. 412.
13. *Orphica, loc. cit.* For additional iconic and literary references, see: W. H. Roscher, ed., *Lexicon der Grieschen und Römischen Mythologie,* Vol. IV (Hildesheim: Georg Olms, 1965), pp. 443–531; *Der Kleine Pauly Lexicon der Antike* (München: Druckenmüller Verlag, 1975), Vol. V. pp. 191ff; James Notopoulos, "Silenos the Scientist," *Classical Journal,* LXII (April 1967), pp. 308f; Karl Kerényi, *Gods of the Greeks* (London: Thames and Hudson, 1974), p. 179, and, *Dionysos: Archetypal Image of the Indestructible Life* (Princeton: Princeton University Press, 1976), pp. 71, 147f, 158, 162, 169, 285, 358f, 367–70, 375–79.
14. Kerényi, "Man and Mask," p. 167.
15. *The Hundred Thousand Songs of Milarepa,* trans. Chang (New York: Harper and Row, 1962), p. 119, *passim.* Marpa, it may be noted in the context of chapter XX, was the founder of a school of Tibetan

Buddhism known as "The *Whispered* Transmission."

16. Alain Daniélou, *Hindu Polytheism* (New York: Pantheon, 1964), p. 91.

17. Cited in: William James, *The Varieties of Religious Experiencd* (New York: Collier Books, 1961), pp. 316, 380. Compare James' own paean to drunkenness: "The sway of alcohol over mankind is unquestionably due to its power to stimulate the mystical faculties of human nature, usually crushed to the earth by the cold facts and dry criticisms of the sober hour. Sobriety diminishes, discriminates, and says no. Drunkenness expands, unites, and says yes" (ibid., p. 304).

18. See: Gerhardus van der Leeuw, *Religion in Essence and Manifestation* (New York: Harper and Row, 1963), vol. II, p. 362.

19. See: Claude Lévi-Strauss, *The Raw and the Cooked* (Introduction to a Science of Mythology, Vol. I), trans. Weightman and Weightman (New York: Harper and Row, 1969), p. 159.

20. Titus 1:3–14; 2:1–15.

21. Hans Jonas, *The Gnostic Religion* (Boston: Beacon Press, 1958), pp. 71ff.

22. *Corpus Hermeticum*, VII.1.

23. *Odes of Solomon*, XI.6–8.

24. *Gospel of Truth*, XXII.13–20.

25. Karl Kerényi, *Dionysos*, pp. 257ff. Joseph Campbell notices the same thing, in: *Masks of God: Creative Mythology* (New York: Viking Press, 1968), p. 26.

26. Jeremiah 2:21. Also, see: Psalm 80:8: "Did thou bring a vine out of Egypt?"

27. Morton Smith, "On the Wine God in Palestine," in: *Salo W. Baron Jubilee Volume* (Jerusalem: American Academy for Jewish Research, 1974), pp. 815ff. Also, see: Smith, *Jesus the Magician* (New York: Harper and Row, 1978), pp. 25, 120. Smith finds special support for his view in: Achilles Tatius, II.ii.1–iii.3.

28. Acts 2:12–15.

29. After completing this work I discovered that Erasmus had long before me proposed the identification of Silenos and Christ in his *Adagia* ("Proverbs"). Ernst Benz has made commentary on this in: "Christus und die Silene des Alcibiades" *Rudolf-Otto-Ehrung* (Berlin: H. Frick, 1940), pp. 1–31; compare Benz' essay, "Christus und Sokrates in der alten Kirche," ZNW XLIII (1950–1951), 195–224.

30. I Corinthians 1:23. Compare, I Corinthians 8:9: "a stumbling block to the weak." If there be any temptation to romanticize drunkenness, any doubt about its pathological nature, a novel by Malcolm Lowry, *Under the Volcano* (New York: New American Library, 1971), will certainly be a proper antidote, even if a sickening one. Also, see the exceptional review of Lowry's work, linking it to the author's own alcoholism, by William Gass, in: *The World within the Word* (New York: Alfred A. Knopf, 1978), pp. 16–38. Gass, for example, comments that this poet's hands were "stained . . . by the masturbation of the bottle (the crystal phallus, in Berryman's phrase)" (p. 24). Also, note Gass' remarkable use of the image of the *cantina* (= "bar," "song," "cave," "deep earthy place," etc.) which corresponds to the image of Silenos' cave in this book. To be sure, the testimony of Lowry and Gass confirm a sense of the pathological nature of Silenic intoxication. Yet, in spite of the negativity, or perhaps just because of the image's dark force, the work of connecting Christ and Silenos holds some promise, as Jung's letter to Freud, cited on p. xxi of the Introduction, implies.

23 Biblical and Theological Drunkenness: The Cases of Lot and Noah

1. Irenaeus, *Against the Heresies*, IV.31.1–2. The Biblical story in question occurs in Genesis 19:30–38, esp. vv. 34ff.

2. Origen, *Contra Celsus*, IV.45.

3. Genesis 9:20f. See the study of the sources on this theme by H. Hirsch Cohen, *The Drunkenness of Noah* (University: Alabama University Press, 1974), *passim*.

4. Origen, *Homily on Genesis*, V. See: Cohen, *op. cit.*, pp. 2ff.

5. Irenaeus, *Against the Heresies*, IV.31f; Origen, *Homily on Genesis*, V. Compare: Cohen, *op. cit.*, chap. I and *passim*.

6. Irenaeus, *Against the Heresies*, IV.31.1–2.

7. Matthew 11:19.

8. Origen, *Homily on Genesis*, V.

9. See: G. W. H. Lampe, ed., *Patristic Greek Lexicon*, fasc. III (Oxford: Clarendon Press, 1964), p. 839.

10. Chrysostom, *Homily on I Timothy*, XIV.6.

11. Origen, *Homily on John*, I.30; Eusebius, *Psalms*, XXII.5; XXXVI.2; Dionysius the Aereopogite, *Epistles*, IX.5; Gregory of Nyssa, *Homily V on Canticles;* Cyril of Jerusalem, *Catechetical Lectures*, XVII.19. Compare: Lampe, ed., *loc. cit.*, and C. G. Jung, *CW*,

XII.177, 182, on the mystical significance of drunkenness in the Orphic and Dionysian religions where the admonition is, *monon mē hydōr*, meaning drink "no water," only wine.

12. Philo, *On Sobriety*, II.

13. Plotinus, *Enneads*, VI.7, 30, 35; V.8, 10; III.5, 9.

14. Plato, *Republic*, IX.573^{b-c}; *Laws*, I.637–665.

15. Cyril of Alexandria, *Amos*, 57.

16. Isaiah 55:10; Psalm 64:10 (LXX)

17. Jeremiah 38:25. On this theme of psychological moistening and Dionysian drunkenness, see: James Hillman, *Myth of Analysis*, pp. 284f.

18. Heraclitus, #36 (Diels-Kranz).

19. Philo, *Plant.*, 162f.

20. Philo, *Vit. mos.*, I.187; II.162.

21. Cyril of Jerusalem, *loc. cit.* For more on the idea of "sober drunkenness," see: E. R. Goodenough, *Jewish Symbols in the Greco-Roman Period*, Vol. XII (New York: Pantheon, 1965), pp. 123–129.

22. In German: *Alles vergängliches / Ist nur ein Gleichnis.* Goethe, *Faust*, II.12104f. Perhaps these lines relate to Philo's sense when he says that the teaching about Noah's drunkenness should be kept secret. (See: Goodenough, *op. cit.*, p. 195.) Metaphor expresses life-meanings indirectly, thereby keeping the significance hidden and obscure—as if it were in Silenos cave!

24 The Poetry of Drunkenness

1. Gerard Manley Hopkins, *Poems and Prose* (Baltimore: Penguin, 1953), p. 67.

2. In German: *Zu der stillen Erde sag: Ich rinne. / Zu dem raschen Wasser sprich: Ich bin.* Rainer Maria Rilke, *Sonnets to Orpheus*, trans. MacIntyre (Berkeley: University of California Press, 1960), II.29 (p. 112). The English translation of MacIntyre reads: "Say unto tranquil earth: I flow. / To the fleeting water speak: I am."

3. John Milton, *Paradise Lost*, Bk. IX.

4. Delmore Schwartz, *Selected Poems: Summer Knowledge* (New York: New Directions, 1967), p. 188. Compare Rilke's lines from a poem about the marriage in Cana. The context is that Mary has urged her son, Jesus, to perform the miracle which would help the host, but she later reflects that this first act of his, which she insisted upon, may have led ineluctably down the road to his ultimate death. The poet writes:

> At table heaped with vegetables and fruits,
> she shared the joy, and never understood
> that the water from her own tear-ducts,
> with this wine, had been transformed into blood.

(*The Life of the Virgin Mary*, trans. Spender [New York: Philosophical Library, 1951], p. 35.) In relation to this stanza note the formulation on page 132, "when he bleeds, it is wine."

5. Martin Heidegger, *Approche de Hölderlin*, trans. Corbin, Deguy, Fedier, and Launay (Paris: Gallimard, 1962), p. 152 (translation from the French by the present author).

6. In the ancient art of alchemy, "fire water" was one of the goals of the work. *The Aurora* says: *ignis noster est aqua* ("our fire is water"). *The Gloria Mundi* tells that "that which unites Sun, Moon, and Mercurius (i.e., body, soul, and spirit) is at once fire and water." *The Rosarium*, Philalethes, and Ripley echo this: "For in our water, fire is sought." For these and other such references, see: C. G. Jung, *CW*, IX.ii.200, 353; XI.354; XII.157 ftn. 31, 336 ftn. 7. Also, see: *Parabola*, III.3 (1978), p. 65, where the phrases, "burning water" and "liquid fire" are cited as descriptions of the sense of things when Mercurius is "animated" (i.e., en-souled) by sulfuric action (e.g., anger). The text here is cited from *Symboles fondamenteaux* by René Guénon. And finally, compare chapter XVII, pp. 99–103, where this same motif was expressed from the perspective of the colors "red" and "white."

7. Gaston Bachelard, *L'Eau et les Rêves* (Paris: Corti, 1971), p. 96, compare pp. 74–79, and all of Chapter II. (Translations by the present author.)

8. Gaston Bachelard, *The Psychoanalysis of Fire*, trans. Ross (Boston: Beacon Press, 1964), p. 92.

9. Cited in: ibid., p. 86. Sucher's work is titled: *Les Sources des merveilleux chez Hoffmann*.

10. Ibid., pp. 83, 85. Compare the poem, "Angel of Time," by Jean-Paul Richter.

25 The Fire in Water: Rhythm's In-between

1. This is poem #33 from the work of 1869, *Petits Poëms en Proses*. The translation is from: Peter Quenell, ed., *The Essence of Baudelaire* (New York: Meridian, 1956), p. 149. Compare other poems of

Baudelaire on this theme: "L'Ame du vin (Le vin des honnêtes gens)"; "Le Vin des Amants"; "Le Vin du solitaire"; etc.

2. Arthur Rimbaud, "A Season in Hell and the Drunken Boat," trans. Varèse (New York: New Directions, 1961), pp. 98, 94f.

3. Paul Verlaine, "Art Poétique," in: Sirich and Barton, eds., *Harper's French Anthology* (New York: Harper and Row, 1935), p. 498.

4. Wallace Stevens, *Collected Poems* (New York: Alfred A. Knopf, 1975), p. 158. Compare the lines by May Swenson: "First I saw the surface, / then I saw it flow, / then I saw the underneath." In: *To Mix with Time* (New York: Scribners, 1963), p. 17.

5. Rilke, *loc. cit.*

6. Ibid., II.1 (p. 56).

7. In German: *"Der Ort des Gedichtes birgt also die Quelle der bewegenden woge das verhülte Wesen desen, was dem metaphysich-äesthetischen Vorstellen zunächst also Rhythmus erscheinen kann."* In: *Unterwegs zur Sprache* (Pfullingen: Neske, 1975), p. 38. The English translation of this appears as: *On the Way to Language,* trans. Hofstadter (New York: Harper and Row, 1971), p. 160, compare p. 149.

8. Victor Zuckerkandl, *Sound and Symbol,* trans. Trask (London: Routledge and Kegan Paul, 1956), p. 169.

9. Ibid., pp. 159, 170, 197.

10. Heraclitus, #67 (Diels-Kranz).

11. For this text, see: Heinrich Zimmer, *Philosophies of India,* ed. Campbell (New York: Meridian Books, 1961), pp. 66–74.

12. Plato, *Republic,* Bk. X.

13. Pascal, *Pensées,* #72.

14. Martin Heidegger, *Existence and Being* (Chicago: Regnery, 1949), p. 288; *Einführung in die Metaphysik* (Tübingen: Niemeyer, 1953), pp. 124f.

15. Martin Heidegger, *Poetry, Language, Thought,* trans. Hofstadter (New York: Harper and Row, 1971), pp. 63f. In German: "Der Ursprung des Kunstwerkes," *Holzwege* (Frankfort: Klosterman, 1950), pp. 51f. Compare: Heidegger, *Discourse on Thinking,* trans. Anderson and Freund (New York: Harper and Row, 1966), *passim.* In German: *Gelassenheit* (Pfullingen: Neske, 1959).

16. Heidegger, *Poetry, Language, Thought,* p. 53 ("Der Ursprung . . . ," pp. 41ff.)

17. Heidegger, *On the Way to Language,* p. 19. (*Unterwegs,* p. 108.)

18. Ibid.

19. Heidegger, *On the Way to Language,* p. 27. (*Unterwegs,* p. 119.)

20. Heidegger, *Poetry, Language, Thought,* pp. 180, 182. In German: *"Das Spiegel-spiel von Welt ist der Reigen des Ereignens. . . . Der Reigen ist der Ring, der ringt, indem er als das Spiegeln spielt* ("Das Ding," *Vorträge und Aufsätze,* Teil II (Pfullingen: Neske, 1967), pp. 53, 55.

21. Heidegger, *On the Way to Language,* p. 106.

22. Heidegger, *Poetry, Language, Thought,* p. 169. ("Das Ding," p. 41.) This intimate relation between "empty" and "full" is also demonstrated, and remarkably so, by William Gass in an essay entitled, "The Ontology of the Sentence" (see: Gass, *op. cit.,* pp. 308–317.)

23. Compare Jung's comments on psyche's rhythms and their connection to erotic sense of meaning (*CW,* V.216–219); Von Franz' observations that man's sense of time is based on rhythm, rather than the reverse (*Number and Time* [Evanston: Northwestern University Press, 1974], pp. 251f, 157f); Rafael Lopez-Pedraza's identification of transference in therapy or in friendship as being located, not in personal meaning, but in the rhythmic flow back and forth between persons (*Hermes and His Children* [Dallas: Spring Publications, 1978], pp. 22f, 27–29); and, Kerényi's naming of the archetypal image of the "between" as Eros Proteurhythmos, a divine child in Greek mythology who creates a world of meaning out of the watery, fluid chaos of psyche's messes by means of music (*Essays on a Science of Mythology,* trans. Hull [New York: Harper and Row, 1963], p. 58). Also, it may be noteworthy in this regard that many heart attacks suffered in middle years are a result, not of blocked arteries, but of disrhythmia, and that it has been found that alcohol makes a cholesterol "sweep" in the physical system which prevents this disrhythmic muscular spasm! (From a private conversation with Dr. William Stewart, neurosurgeon, Syracuse, New York.)

26   The Water of Fire: An Art of Forgetting

1. From the text of the opera by Jules Barbier and Michel Carré.

2. Rilke, *Duino Elegies,* trans. Leishman and Spender (New York: Norton, 1963), II.63 (pp. 32f).

3. Rilke, *Sonnets,* II.16 (pp. 86ff).

4. In the Ox-Herding Pictures of Shobun (15th Century), which reproduce Kaku-an's Pictures, the Tenth Picture has a man carrying a wine gourd. This is said to symbolize both a wine-bottle, that is, drunkenness, and *sunyātā,* the Buddhist goal of "emptiness." See: D. T. Suzuki, *Manual of Zen Buddhism* (New York: Grove Press,

1960), p. 134, ftn. 1; and, D. R. Otsu, *The Ox and his Herdsman,* trans. Trevor (Tokyo: Hokuseido, 1969), p. 23 ftn. Also, recall the famous Eighteenth-Century Buddhist artist, Wang Hsia, who always painted while drunk. (See: Conrad Hyers, *Zen and the Comic Spirit* [London: Rider, 1974], p. 51.)

5. See: Robert Payne, ed., *The White Pony: An Anthology of Chinese Poetry* (New York: Mentor Books, 1974), pp. 129–131.

6. Ibid., p. 135.

7. Ibid., p. 142.

8. Ibid., p. 138.

9. Ibid., p. 143.

10. Ibid., p. 144.

11. See, for example: Gerhard Adler, "Remembering and Forgetting," *Panarion 1976* (Tape Recording, C. G. Jung Institute, 12301 Wilshire Blvd., Los Angeles, CA 90025); Mircea Eliade, "Mythologies of Memory and Forgetting," in: *Myth and Reality* (New York: Harper and Row, 1963), Chap. VII; Martin Nilsson, "Die Quellen der Lethe und der Mnemosyne," *Eranos 12–1943*, pp. 62ff, which is responded to by Kerényi, in: "Mnemosyne—Lesmosyne: Über die Quellen 'Erinnerung' und 'Vergessenheit,'" a translation of which appears in: *Spring 1977* (Dallas), pp. 120ff.

12. Perhaps the best reading of this language-fantasy is that of Martin Heidegger. For example, see: "Aletheia (Heraklit Frag. 16)," in: *Vorträge und Aufsätze,* Teil III (Pfullingen: Neske, 1967), pp. 60–62, *passim.* In English: *Early Greek Thinking,* trans. Krell and Capuzzi (New York: Harper and Row, 1975), pp. 108f, *passim.* Here Heidegger writes: "We act as if forgetting (*epilanthanesthai*) were the most transparent thing in the world. Only fleetingly does anyone notice that there is a reference to 'remaining concealed' in the corresponding Greek word (*lanthanomai*). But what does 'forgetting' mean? Modern man, who puts all his stock into forgetting as quickly as possible, certainly ought to know what it is. But he does not. He has forgotten the essence of forgetting, assuming he ever thought about it fully, i.e., thought it out within the essential sphere of oblivion. The continuing indifference toward the essence of forgetting does not result simply from the superficiality of our contemporary way of life. What takes place in such indifference comes from the essence of oblivion itself. It is inherent in it to withdraw itself and to founder in the wake of its own concealment. The Greeks experienced oblivion, *lēthē,* as a destiny of concealment. . . . When we forget, something doesn't just slip away from us. Forgetting itself slips into a concealing, and indeed in such a way that we ourselves, along with our relation to what is forgot-

ten, fall into concealment ... Both in the way the Greek employs *lanthanein*, 'to remain concealed,' as a basic and predominant verb, as well as in the experience of the forgetting or remaining-concealed, this much is made sufficiently clear: *lanthanō*, 'I remain concealed,' does not signify just a form of human behavior among many others, but identifies the basic trait of every response to what is present or absent—if not, indeed, the basic trait of presence and absence themselves." Compare, James Hillman on *Lēthē*, in: "Dream and the Underworld," *Eranos 42–1973* (Leiden: Brill, 1975), pp. 313ff.

13. See: Eric Partridge, *Origins* (New York: Macmillan, 1958), p. 253.

27 The Arrow of Intoxication and the Nick of Time

1. Luke 17:22–34.
2. Mark 10:17; Luke 18:18; John 15:1.
3. Luke 17:33.
4. Aeschylus, *Agamemnon*, 363ff. See: R. B. Onians, *The Origins of European Thought* (New York: Arno, 1973), pp. 373ff. I am indebted to Onians for the research which follows.
5. Euripides, *Suppliants*, 745f.
6. Homer, *Iliad*, IV.185; VIII.84f, 325f; XI.439.
7. *Odyssey*, XIX.573ff; and, Judges 4:21. See: Onians, *op. cit.*, p. 347.
8. Compare: Jung, *CW*, XIV.190: "If you will contemplate your lack of fantasy, of inspiration and inner aliveness, which you feel as sheer stagnation and a barren wilderness, and impregnate it with the interest born of alarm at your inner death, then something can take shape in you, for your inner emptiness conceals just as great a fullness if only you will allow it to penetrate into you." Jung had written earlier about this notion in the privately published booklet, *Septem Sermones ad Mortuos* ("Seven Sermons to the Dead"): "I begin with nothingness. Nothingness is the same as fullness. In infinity full is no better than empty. Nothingness is both empty and full. ... This nothingness or fullness we name Pleroma. ... Because we are parts of the pleroma, the pleroma is also in us. ... The empty-fullness of the whole is the pleroma." (See: *Memories, Dreams, Reflections* [New York: Vintage Books, 1965], pp. 379, 385.)
9. Pierre Nautin, in fact, shows how Origen, for one, never viewed things according to the preaching/teaching split. He quotes Origen's *Homilies*, XX.vi.21; XIX.xiv.108; and, XV.ii.8, as saying in effect: "The role of the teacher is to convert, that is, to move the student's soul."

See: Nautin, "Origène prédicateur," in: *Origène homélies sur Jérémie, I-II*, ed. Nautin, *Sources chrétiennes*, 232 (Paris: Editions du Cerf, 1976), p. 152. Not only does Origen affirm the intimate link between preaching and teaching in the case of the Great Teacher, but language itself expresses a further connection between drunkenness and the life of preaching/teaching. The terms for preaching in both French (*prêcher*) and German (*predigen*) are rooted in a Latin word which gives to English its word, "addiction." *Prêcher* is from the Latin, *praedicator, praedicāre*, meaning "to proclaim." The base of this is *dēdicāre*, meaning "to consecrate to the gods" and "to declare solemnly" (the "de-" prefix being an intensifier). *Predigen* has its root in the same stem. The stem, in turn, gives English the term, "addict," that is, *addictus*, meaning "assigned by decrees, bound, devoted" (being the past participle of *addicēre* from *ad* = "to" + *dicēre* = "to say"). So, the uses of "addiction" moved from original theological to later secular realms of life, the earliest of these uses referring to an "addiction" to God of which the later use, "addiction" to drink or drug, is a metaphor of the religious meaning. That is, it is *not* the case that the meaning, "addiction to God," is a metaphor of "addiction to drink." For example, in an English translation of Titus 1:1 (1549), we read: "I Paule my selfe ye addict servant and obeyer . . . of God ye father." In Fuller's *Church History* (1655), there is a similar use of the term: "We sincerely addict ourselves to Almighty God." These uses correspond to that of Shakespeare, for example, in *II Henry IV*, IV.iii.135: "To forsweare thine Potations, and to addict themselves to Sack." Also, compare the common way of ending letters in the sixteenth and seventeenth centuries, as for example in this case from Thomas Moorly: "And so I rest, In all love and affection to you, Most addicted . . . etc."

10. Recall the comment of William Blake who, one year before his death, wrote in a friend's autograph album: "William Blake, born 28 November 1757, in London, and has died several times since."

INDEX

195